Ple

Renewals c
by internet
in person
by phone

HOMELESS CHILD.
GROOMED GIRL.
TEENAGE PROSTITUTE.

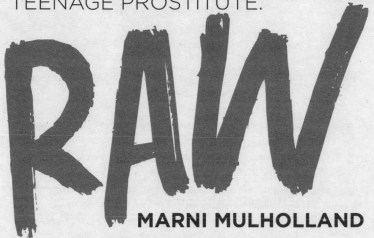

MARNI MULHOLLAND

EBURY
PRESS

5 7 9 10 8 6

First published in 2014 by Ebury Press, an imprint of Ebury Publishing
A Random House Group company

The Random House Group Limited Reg. No. 954009

Addresses for companies within the Random House Group can be found at
www.randomhouse.co.uk

A CIP catalogue record for this book is available from the British Library

The Random House Group Limited supports the Forest Stewardship
Council® (FSC®), the leading international forest-certification organisation.
Our books carrying the FSC label are printed on FSC®-certified paper. FSC is
the only forest-certification scheme supported by the leading environmental
organisations, including Greenpeace. Our paper procurement policy can be
found at www.randomhouse.co.uk/environment

Printed and bound by CPI Group (UK) Ltd, Croydon, CR0 4YY

ISBN 9780091957841

To buy books by your favourite authors and register for offers visit
www.randomhouse.co.uk

*'Speak up for those who cannot
speak for themselves.'*

PROVERBS 31:8

How does it start? A look, a smile, a laugh, a hug, a play, a game. A cuddle, a fumble, a touch. Reassurance. A finger. Lubrication. Another finger. Lick. 'Do you like that, little one?' Another. 'You do, don't you?' Then out comes an almighty snake. 'Look! Here is my snake, he's awake! Do you want to touch him? Don't be scared...' He loses himself, progressing to full-on penetration. The snake spits and she splits.

'I couldn't help myself!' he cries. Looking down at what he's done, he's horrified, but only for a second. He liked it, he's hooked and he knows he will do it again.

The little girl thinks: *This isn't new to me. It's been done before. It's what all 'daddies' do.*

I became a victim of a paedophile who smelt of Fisherman's Friends.

Grooming happened to me.

ONE

'Train up a child in the way he should go:
and when he is old, he will not depart from it.'

PROVERBS 22:6

Rumble, rumble, rumble
Notting Hill, February 1976

On tippy toes, I pressed our buzzer with my long finger. *When I am six I am sure to grow.* I pressed again. No answer. *Where's my mummy?* A big plank laid across the door with some kind of note on it. I pressed harder, with my thumb this time. Nothing. I got bored and played hopscotch, fiddled with my hair, sang a song and felt my tummy rumble. *Rumble, rumble, rumble, in the jungle.* I jumped from one paving stone to another, carefully missing the cracks in the pavement, otherwise I'd be swallowed up by a large worm. *Yuck!*

I played the counting game. *One, two red cars. One, two, three blue cars. One, two sparkly cars.* And one filthy white van full of furniture, with my dad's scraggy younger brother Danny yelling at me to, 'Stop pricking around and sit your arse down on that sofa in the back before I smack it.' So the silly leprechaun could take me to my new period dwelling in Chelsea.

There'd be no more fleeing over rooftops in pyjamas because of scraps that broke out in the stairwell: thumping, fighting, shouting, screaming 'Plastic Paddy!', the insult for people that pretended to be Irish, but weren't.

I was second generation Irish but liked by neither the Irish nor the English. My mother maintained the Irish hated us for leaving and the bastard English never forgave us for arriving. That was obvious: if yet another bomb went off in London, I'd always take the blame. 'Potato head,' they called me at school. No one would include me in a *Charlie's Angels* game for a few days, but they soon forgot, and I'd play Farrah Fawcett once again.

It didn't help when they found out I had the same surname as a famous Fenian family. That all but killed my popularity. Lucky for me and my mother that we were the same colour as the English. As long as she kept her mouth shut when we ventured out, our heritage was invisible and we were left alone.

I was so proud of my mother: she was beautiful then. 'Ahhh, your ma is the image of Brigitte Bardot, so she is,' Uncle Danny would say to me – he was always the exaggerator. He had a soft spot for her, seeing as his brother had left her in the lurch. She had a pout and long, golden-brown hair that we could all sit on. Skirts that skimmed the pavement; my first vague memory is of her looking ethereal in a floaty number. Rifling through racks of ruffled dresses, while I sat in my buggy beside the wide sweeping stairs of a store in darkness, admiring the colourful heels of hippies who browsed. My mother walked into Biba in an old dress and walked straight out with a new one underneath.

I lost a Start-rite on the way out. I'd kicked it off in Kensington, but she didn't notice till Chelsea. I was inconsolable, my mother amused. She was on a high from her non-purchase.

'What an adventure!' she giggled, hurrying down the Kings Road.

Our new flat had Georgian charm with a practical layout, spoilt by a bathroom floor caved in from subsidence. But it was quieter, smarter, altogether nicer than Notting Hill. At night, from the tall slim windows of the living room, we could look out at the lights of the Albert Bridge, count how many bulbs needed replacing, see the Thames glistening, whether the tide was high or low. I was afraid the river might spill over, come and get me.

As we walked the surrounding streets of an afternoon, my mother liked to point out the fancy buildings and comment on the plush furnishings through the windows. 'Would you look at that scrumptious squashy sofa and that gorgeous baby grand!' she'd say. 'Do ya think they'd mind if we moved in, Marni?' she'd mess.

Even though we were living in a tumbledown council flat and our Laura Ashley curtains were second hand, my mum made an effort with the interior. We had rugs on bare boards, globe paper lanterns, bamboo shelves, wicker chairs, potted palms and an open fire. She might have been stylish, but she was also a right bloody snob.

'Not dirty, disgusting *toilet*,' she cried to me. 'Call it the loo! Loo! Loooooo!' When she wasn't hyper like this, she'd be aloof, waltzing around the flat with her nose in the air singing 'Hey Mr Tambourine Man, all men must be destroyed' to the tune of the Bob Dylan song, while she plaited her very fine hair. I was confused by these words, I didn't understand.

'Everything is fine,' she shrilled when I asked her. It was her mantra. She drummed it into me, 'Repeat after me, "Everything is fine".'

'Everything is fine,' I echoed, trying to please.

On her up days, my mother loved to roam. I'd be shunted out of bed and taken to bizarre places at sunrise.

'Get up, get up!' she'd cry. 'We're going on an adventure.'

We'd walk – or rather skip – all the way to anywhere. We'd run over the Albert Bridge, climb over railings and race through Battersea Park, dropping pennies from our pockets while rolling down grassy slopes, then losing ourselves in the adventure playground. We'd play hide and seek among the trees, then wait an age for a bus to take us to Trafalgar Square, at a time when I should really have been going to school. My mum would often drift off into her own private world while crouching there by the bus stop. She'd be miles away, humming to herself, not feeling me tug on her corduroy skirt, not hearing me ask, 'Mummy, Mummy, is this our bus?' when it had come to a halt right in front of us. Eventually she'd register and leap up like a frog.

'Quick, quick, or we'll *miss* it!' she'd scream.

When we arrived at our destination, we tried to climb the three lions without success, then ended our tour at St Pancras, all before 9 a.m. 'Isn't it glorious?' my mum would gush, pointing out the 'fine architecture' of the station roof. It looked filthy to me.

Then we'd take the train down to Brighton for a fried doughnut on the pier. As I licked the sugar from the sides of my mouth, I looked through the cracks in the floor and froze as the sea raged below. *So close!* My fear was soon forgotten as we took a flutter on the slot machines, a slide on the helter-skelter and a ride on the carousel, with my mother sitting side-saddle.

'Woo-hoo!' she hollered, as her skirt went over her head. Then we scrabbled over humongous pebbles on the beach to a wooden shack, bought a stick of rock with someone else's name running through it, and skipped back to our train, where we hid in the loo and giggled when we heard the guard walk past shouting, 'Tickets please!' My mother never ever paid the fare for the ride back home.

On a Saturday, she'd take a pitch in Portobello. I'd be counting down the days to the weekend, I loved the market so much. 'It's Wednesday, only three sleeps to go-o-o!' I'd think. We'd wake with the bin men and get the number 31 bus up to Notting Hill.

When the buildings got scruffy I knew we were there. We'd queue for a stall in the Good Fairy Market so my mother could sell the bits and bobs she had brought in her wheelie. We would wait for what felt like ten hours, playing hopscotch and singing, 'We all live in a tub of margarine,' irritating the hell out of those who knew the real words of the Beatles song. Finally, she was given a space to put out her marcasite, lazulite and coral necklaces and earrings on a large linen tablecloth.

I'd cosy on down under the stall, wrapped in my coat. I'd lie on empty bags and study the shoes of tourists shopping. Lots of platforms, I noticed, with the occasional clogs and Jesus sandals. Never any socks. A pram would go by and I'd find myself locking eyes with a toddler. I'd make a silly face to make them laugh, but all they'd do was cry. I'd be right up close to a handbag or two; it would have been so easy to pinch a purse. What stopped me was an order to, 'Get up and go get the tea.'

I'd write down the orders from the other stallholders and skip up to the corner of the Grove to a unit squeezed between a lady selling lamps and a man polishing big brass things. A girl marked the number of sugars on the polystyrene teacups in biro. Balancing them on top of each other, I'd walk back very slowly, making sure they didn't topple. I liked having a purpose.

I'd eat a crusty cheddar roll with the offending slices of tomato flicked out. Then I'd go for a wander through the crowds, past the antique stalls, through the fruit and veg bit, ending up outside the Electric Cinema. The stallholders all knew me, pinching my ruddy cheeks as I strode past.

'What a munchkin!' they'd say. *What a pain!* I'd think. I'd stick my tongue out, then scarper round the back past the Tabernacle, the church that had become a community centre, and find myself parallel to Portobello. I played on the swings then looked over at a huge pile of rubble and realised I was in the very square where our old house had once stood. I danced around hoping I'd catch the eye of someone I knew. But the truth was, I bumped into more of my friends in Chelsea now. Most of them had been rehoused in the humongous red-brick estate down by the Thames.

The council had once offered us a flat in that estate. 'On a dangerously high floor,' my mother had bleated, appalled. The flat was practically in the sky. It had central heating, new windows and a bath that wasn't even in the kitchen; it was in its very own room, all shiny, new and clean. But my mother refused to take it. *Shame, I thought, I could have had so much fun with that lift.* Instead, we were the last ones to leave our scruffy square. We squatted with cockroaches in a building that was beautiful but condemned, all because she didn't want to accept anything modern. 'I like a house with a touch of character,' she told the housing officer, 'with an architrave perhaps, and fine cornicing. Oh, and it must have high ceilings,' she added. 'I can't help being partial to a bit of Georgian. Ireland was full of it, you know.'

I'm surprised he didn't say, 'Well, bog off back there then!'

When we had a rare bit of money, we'd meet rellies at the Troubadour on the Old Brompton Road. I'd get cuddles and lots of 'love ya's then gobble carrot cake. Or the pair of us would scoff pancakes full of cream at Asterix on the Kings Road, while my mother tapped the table like a piano as she listened to some concerto they were playing. It made a change from the norm, eating beans from a tin. We never had any food in the flat, but that was okay because I got free school milk, served warm with a stripy straw that I'd splatter all over my glasses.

Whether they were shattered, stamped on or bent, I always wore my specs. Perched at an odd angle on the end of my nose and held together with sticky tape, which caught and pulled single hairs out of my head every time I moved. Pale eyes always squinting, I was as blind as a bat. I felt so helpless when they fell off, or were knocked off by some little cow at school who then refused to give them back.

'Over here, yer blind Paddy!' The girl shrieked with laughter when I ran in the direction of her voice and fell into the sand pit.

I was disabled without them. I needed my bottle tops to understand. I relied on watching people's mouths move, more than I would have liked. Was that unusual? I wondered if there were more like me. Was I deaf as well as blind? I kept that worry to myself. There would be no hearing aid for me, I was bullied enough because of my comedy glasses.

Cigarettes and orange Smarties

My glasses had been broken a long time when I skipped across the road to play with my little neighbour with an Alice band in her nicely brushed hair. We looked so like each other, we could have been twins. Blue eyes, wispy blonde hair, long skinny legs. She lived in an identical house to mine, only she had the whole place, all freshly painted with flowers on the window sills. She had a lovely sunny bedroom covered in spongy thick carpet I could roll on all day, dotty wallpaper that made my eyes goggle, and her room was *full* of teddies. Teddies on the bed playing, teddies under the bed hiding, teddies in the bed sleeping. She had *everything*, a massive doll's house – even a dad. He didn't fit in the doll's house, though.

Why had my mother and I been given a flat so close to the rich? If we had been housed with the poor, I wouldn't have known what I was missing. Often I would look out through my window into Little Miss Alice Band's, wishing we could swap our lives. But not our mummies. Hers was dead boring compared to mine. I loved my mum, even though she was a bit scary.

I'd been inside my neighbour's house loads of times, but today she wouldn't let me in.

'My daddy told me that we are not to play together any more,' she said, 'because you're not our sort.' I didn't understand, neither did she by the confused look on her face. 'My daddy says you're poor,' she explained, 'and worse, you're Irish.'

I wish she'd had a sign up outside her house saying, *Friends wanted. Irish need not apply.* She'd have saved me a lot of heartache. *Am I bad?* I thought. For the first time ever, I felt crap about myself and that little girl superior. It was a long walk home, eleven steps across the road to a funny mummy and some yucky custard. At least I had my Lego. I loved Lego, making things, usually houses. Or a garage for Daddy's car; he might come and see me then.

Teary, I moped down the river, to see a cousin who lived in a tiny flat way up high in that vast red-brick estate. He bounced off the walls and refused to eat anything but orange Smarties and cigarettes. His mother grabbed his arm, held him down and fished those fags out of his mouth yelling, 'You're very bold!' to his great distress. I couldn't wait to leave, however great the view.

From then on, when Little Miss Alice Band ignored me in the street and went off to play with her sort in their private garden square, I always thought of my little cousin. What hope did he have high up on the 18th floor? Less than me in the pristine streets of Chelsea. Having rich neighbours, however snooty, was not the worse thing in the world. *I'm so lucky to live on a street and not trapped up high. There's always a child worse off than me*, I thought, while finishing off creamed rice in a tin.

Earls Court, 27 March 1976
A device explodes in a rubbish bin; a young man loses his hearing in one ear. He's bleeding but dares not ask for help, slipping quietly from the mayhem.

*He's in pain but steers clear of hospital for fear of
opening his mouth. He'll give himself away. Another
Irish Catholic, the enemy. This man I do not know
is my father.*

My uncle Danny was often at our flat, sniffing around,
as he had no wife or kids of his own. He'd turn up in his
battered white van and prickly red beard with a rickety
table or some other tat he'd found for my mother. 'I
bought it from the auction, antique so it is,' he'd
announce, his grimy jeans falling off his skinny frame. It
was very hard not to look at the crease of his puny arse
on full show, he really did need a belt.

'Ahh, I'm only pulling your leg now,' he admitted,
while struggling to heave the wreck out. 'I found it in a
skip.' With his back bent double he seemed so feeble, he
must have been runt of the litter. I'm sure puffing on a
horrid pipe didn't help.

But Uncle Danny was so much fun, always the joker.
Locked in a room that he'd just done a big smelly in, I
could hear his keys jangling from his belt loop while he
tried to stifle his giggles. On a double-decker bus he'd tie
my hair to a rail, so I couldn't get off. I missed my stop
and had to walk back, only to witness him roaring with
laughter. I roared too.

Seeing me shiver, he wrapped his *Starsky and Hutch*-
style knitted cardy round me. With his triangular
eyebrows raised, his piercing blue eyes stared up into
the sky. 'You know, Marni,' he whispered, giving me a

cuddle. 'I have jumped from one fluffy cloud to another and actually tasted them. They're just like candyfloss.'

After spag bol in the Chelsea Kitchen, we trundled off to Woolies where he showed me how to steal penny sweets, then made them disappear behind his ear. In Soho he asked me, 'Will ya ever be giving us 50 pence now?' so he could have a little peek in a shop with a blacked-out window, while I sat for an age on the doorstep.

'Love ya!' he shouted, giving me a scratchy wet kiss and vanishing behind a purple crushed velvet curtain. What was he doing in there? I knew it was naughty, but I didn't know why. It scared me. Was he ever coming back? Waiting, waiting, waiting. That first feeling of panic.

At the Silver Jubilee he lifted me high on to his shoulders to escape the crowds in Piccadilly, while proudly singing anti-loyalist songs:

> *When boyhood's fire was in my blood I read of*
> *   ancient freemen,*
> *For Greece and Rome who bravely stood,*
> *Three hundred men and three men;*
> *And prayed I yet might see our fetters rent in twain,*
> *And Ireland, long a province, be a nation once again.*
> *A nation once again, a nation once again,*
> *And Ireland, long a province, be a nation once again.*

Then he was gone.

Crab
August 1977

We went to see Grandma in the holidays. The long train journey to tumbleweed, so tedious to a child full of energy. A notebook, felt tips. There was only so much I could draw, play hangman, go to the loo and lose at noughts and crosses while sucking a soggy sarnie wrapped in cling film. I looked out of the window and saw the landscape change from grey flats to green fields, just like Ireland.

The food trolley rattled through, shelves stuffed full of temptation on the same level as my face. A Twix, a Flake, a Kit Kat. *Mm-mm*, I thought, smelling them. I wanted that Kitty Kat so badly, but had no money for treats. I had a strong urge to steal, but knew I was not supposed to. Besides, there were far too many grown ups about me, so I didn't. *Shame the people are not asleep, I'd have the Twix, two Flakes and five whole Kit Kats! Then I'd break those Kit Kats up into fingers and create a scaffold of chocolate. Then, slowly, one by one from the bottom, I'd pull out each finger till the whole thing fell. Then I'd eat it. That would while away at least 20 minutes.*

Instead, I sat on my hands and waited till the sweets went away. At least I'd have a meal at Grandma's.

'Are we there yet?' I asked, over and over, kicking the seat in front. I was impatient to board the bus to her house.

'Now remember,' my mother said, 'don't talk about the Troubles. The English killing the Irish is a banned subject. You never know who's listening,' she whispered loudly. I didn't understand 'the Troubles', neither did I care. Bombs rarely went off now anyway, that's what my mother told me when I got the fear and started to understand my own mortality.

All I could think about was my holiday in the suburbs where the Irish had settled, the home of my family. Endless cousins to play with, strawberries to pick, trees to climb, rose petals to squash and sniff, worms to dig and cut in half. There would be freshly baked scones to eat, lemonade to drink and Mars Bars to store for the return journey home.

On Holy Day, families were trussed up in their Sunday best and took the long walk to church. I always remained five paces behind, I didn't have the right clothes. These places of worship grandma would take me to were bursting with the atmosphere of a street party. Guitars, flutes and singing, loud from the soul. I sang nothing, I stayed at the back, I was not one of them, it made no difference my passport was green. The collection basket was passed from pew to pew, full of coins. I sat on my hands again.

We ran on to a bus that then must have stopped 100 times on its way to a bleak area, where we found Grandma and a bear of a man she had staying with her.

The Bear bent down to kiss me. I looked into his deep-set grey eyes, touched his face and melted as he grinned.

'Hello there!' he said, his accent a singsong to my ears. He turned on the radio. A grown-up person's station playing Chris de Burgh. I listened while he sat down and read his paper.

I was staying with Grandma for weeks and weeks while my mother went home. Grandma was relatively young with a strong constitution, which meant she still had the energy for the likes of skinny me.

'I'll be taking great care of her,' she said to my mother, not that she was listening, her head swaying, lost in her own world as usual. 'She'll not be a bother,' Grandma went on, patting my head. 'She's my pet.'

There was much more structure at Grandma's post-war house than there ever was at home. Meals came every day, there were hot baths with bubbles and nice shampoo. Afterwards, bundled up in a clean towel with my hair all squeaky, the tips of my fingers soft and wrinkly, I insisted Grandma read my *Famous Five* book that I'd brought, 'all the way from London'. We'd have three whole chapters of Julian, Dick, Anne, George and Timmy getting into all sorts of adventures with a boat. Then, 'Bed!' she cried.

That ten seconds before sleep, pillow just right. Mmm, I'm all cosy.

I slept in the very same room my mother had slept in as a teenager, with its threadbare carpet and Crittall window. The same patterned paper and faded curtains. The same narrow bed, with the soft mattress she had once shared with her sisters, with her brothers in the room next door. The Bear was in there now. I could hear him snoring at night when I should have been asleep. He stopped after a while. I wondered if my grandma went in and turned him over. Now he was awake. He stood at my door and said, 'Night, night.'

A cheap painting of a young girl in knee-high socks hung wonky on the wall. She had tears in the corner of her big blue eyes. Eyes that followed me everywhere. I wondered what that young girl had seen in this little box bedroom over the years. *I wish you could talk to me. What was my mother like? Did she giggle like I do? Not sleep when she was supposed to? Stay up to be alone? Your tears look very real, are you not happy?*

After the excitement of the first few days, Grandma became rather cold and distant. She took the bus into town, leaving me on my own with the Bear. What was she thinking as she walked off smiling, waving at us through the window? Did she carry on smiling when I could see her no more?

I knew that leaving me behind with him got me out of her hair. I slowed her down when she was running her errands, she had told me so. 'You're always skipping instead of walking, stopping and staring at toy shops.' Anyway, I had the Bear to muck about with.

I turned to him, clapped my hands and said, 'Let's play!' At his invitation, I sat on his lap. But not in the same way I'd sat on Santa's lap last Christmas at the school jumble sale. He made me face him, legs on either side. Tapping on my knee he sang:

There was an old woman, who swallowed a fly.

Then he started circling the inside of my thigh.

I don't know why, she swallowed a fly.
Perhaps she'll die.

Slowly he stroked me, from the bottom of my leg all the way to the top, his fingers circling as he sang:

There was an old woman, who swallowed a spider,
That wriggled and tickled and jiggled inside her.

He spilt his water in all the excitement, over my skirt and knickers.

'Now be a good girl and take your wet things off,' he said, 'so we can dry them.'

Humming to myself, I took them off, and he spread them carefully on a radiator that wasn't even on.

'Open your legs,' he said, 'so I can clean you up.' He wiped me between my legs with a cloth, lingering just a little with his big hairy hands. 'Wider, now, wider,' he ordered. My knees were almost touching my ears.

He asked me to do handstands, cartwheels, and his favourite, a 'crab'. I'd start by kneeling, legs apart, leaning back, raising my hips. Arching, stretching up, with the help of my hands for balance. My legs would be splayed with everything else in between. He'd make me do a crab over and over, until I could stay in position up to the count of ten.

'One! Two! Three! Four! Five! Six! Seven! Eight!

Nine! Nine and a half... Ten!' It was tiring. He stood there staring with his mouth wide open. He started to fidget. Playfully, he smacked my bottom when I stood up. And told me I was 'very bold'.

'I'd like to be your da,' he said, hugging me again, 'so I could play with you all the time.'

That would be nice, I thought. To have him as a daddy, even though he was old. He lifted me on to his scraggy shoulders and skipped around the room, my thighs now rubbing the back of his neck. Then he twisted me round, so his mouth was facing my fanny. He lifted me up a little and started blowing big strong raspberries on to me. I screamed with delight, it tickled so much. I held on to his grey hair, begging for more, pulling harder and harder, pushing his head closer. Long wet raspberries.

'It feels funny!' I cried.

He continued until he was red in the face. He then pulled away. Soaked with his saliva, he wanted me to play fight, rough and tumble over the floor. He threw me around and my face ended up between his legs. There was a big bulge in his trousers. Without thinking, I patted it.

Now we played horsey horsey. I sat spread-eagled on him and started rocking.

'Yee-haw!' I cried. I threw my head back and giggled. Rocking, rocking, rocking. He grabbed my hips suddenly and placed me right on top of his bulge, holding me firmly in place. He pushed me back and forth, back and forth. Faster and faster. It was odd but it felt nice. I liked this game.

'Yee-haw!' he copied, croaking out the word excitedly. Then he stopped. 'Look what you've made me do,' he said, crossly. He was wet, on the zip fastening of his trousers. Must have been from the water. Out of breath, he said without looking at me, 'Be off with you. I'm tired and need a rest.'

I was upset. I'd made him angry and I didn't know why. We'd just been having fun. I ran upstairs to my room with the wonky portrait.

Young girl with tears in the corner of your big blue eyes, what have I done wrong?

But I got excited thinking about him playing horsey with me again. I liked that feeling between my legs, that unfamiliar throb. It made me want to wriggle. Later that night I put a pillow between my legs and started rubbing, trying hard to recreate that tingling. He was so smiley and cuddly. Is this what all men did? Is this how they all played? I hoped so.

I want to do it again!

God's helper
October 1979

My mother graduated from her stall in Portobello to a shop off the Fulham Road. It was a short-lived enterprise, but I enjoyed loitering in the window on a Saturday in a second-hand chair. On full display. Until some creep came in and asked, 'Is *she* for sale?'

Some weekends I'd stay at home, then wish I hadn't as all that was on was the racing. But often I had no choice; I'd wake and my mum would be gone. Sometimes it felt as if I didn't have a mum any more.

To pass the hours till she came home I taught myself to swim. I was not going to be afraid of the river any more. Or the sea. So I took myself off to the baths by the Town Hall, slipped under the barrier, changed, padded past all the mummies and daddies and children on tippy toes for fear of getting a verruca, and hesitantly entered the shallow kids' pool.

Push myself off the side, wave my arms around and KICK!

I kept repeating these same movements over and over, sinking to the bottom each time. I noticed the other kids had orange armbands, Snoopy rubber rings, bright blue floats. Their dads coached them while their mums held them. *How would they ever learn?*

One day my determination worked. It was holiday mayhem in there, so no one noticed as I made it to the other side with my feet not once touching the bottom. No one cared as I pulled myself out grinning with pride. As I peeled off my mock Speedo cozzie in the changing room and pulled on my twisted knickers, I was pretty pleased with myself. I decided to celebrate by stealing a tiny chocolate egg covered in shiny foil on the way out. I sucked it while swinging my dripping wet cozzie round and round above my head all the way home. I couldn't wait till the evening to tell my mum, but I knew she'd not make a fuss. She'd just hum and plait her hair. These days she was more angry than happy. I didn't know why, she wasn't really looking after me any more. There was never any friendly Irish banter coming from her. No cakes, no biscuits, no 'craic'. No visits from callers were ever repeated, apart from one.

My day of being home alone listening to 'The Tide Is High' on the radio was interrupted by one of the helpers from the local church doing his rounds. He was dropping in on the fragile and the needy for a cup of tea and hopefully a moist piece of cake. Lemon cake, drizzle cake, chocolate cake, always wanting the cake.

'I am weary,' he said, as I pushed open the door, 'will you not let me in?'

I was nervous as I had only ever seen God's helper behind church walls. He was a powerful being who prayed in the front pew with his head bowed low. When I went up for Communion, I would feel him watching me through his curly hair when I stuck my tongue out, waiting for the priest to place 'the body of Christ' in my mouth. Then I'd close my eyes and taste the wafer. It was crispy till I made it soft with my saliva and swallowed it whole. I always wanted more. I'd go up twice for the craic with that man's eyes glued to me, but he never told on me.

After Mass, he crouched down so his face was the same level as mine and whispered 'Hello'. I could see his eyes, he wasn't so scary now. He gave me six Jammie Dodgers in the vestibule and watched me enjoying them. Slowly nibbling at the shortbread first, I gave him my best sideways smile and said, 'I always save the sticky stuff till last.'

'So do I!'

Finally I let him in to the flat. It was messy, as always. Looking about him, he found a chair in a corner and plonked himself down.

'Here, come sit on my lap,' he said.

'I don't want to,' I replied shyly, my hand over my mouth.

Carefully he took it away. 'Come up, come on,' he said.

Slowly I climbed on, sucking my hair. His legs were bony.

'Now, can you do a Hail Mary for me?' he asked.

'I don't want to,' I mumbled, my hand back over my mouth.

'Come on.'

'Hail-Mary-full-of-grace,' I gasped out. 'The-Lord-is-with-thee,' I managed to add, as he opened my legs and wet me with his saliva. 'Blessed-art-thou-among-women.' I closed my eyes and bit my lip. 'And-blessed-is-the-fruit-of-thy-womb-Jesus,' I yelped, as he touched me.

He joined in. 'Holy Mary, Mother of God, pray for us sinners, now and at the hour of our death,' he intoned. 'Amen.'

He was breathing heavily.

'Again!' he ordered. 'Again!'

I remember his glee and my fear. *There-is-always-a-child-worse-off-than-me*. I thought. That little phrase kept my spirits up.

He groaned, I didn't know why. Then he smiled. 'You're a very bad girl,' he said. 'Now make sure you go to confession.'

It was quiet in the church. Dark in the confession box. I could hear the priest panting through the grill. Smell him too, wafts of old bacon.

'I am very sorry,' I said, 'but I have nothing to confess.'

'Do not try to perfume your flesh,' the priest replied, 'you tempt others into forbidden vice. A very sinful girl. Now pray ten Hail Marys and may God forgive you!'

God's helper was the only visitor who ever wanted to come again. Surprising given there was only a tomato in the fridge and certainly no cake.

Cabbage and crispy potatoes
October 1981

I paid for food in the supermarket with my mum's cheque that she knew would bounce, which I'd see pinned on the wall of shame by the till if I ever dared go in there again.

'Everything is fine,' my mum would shrill, when it clearly wasn't. I was bloody hungry.

I turned up at friends' houses hoping I might get something to eat. I started to choose my friends by who had the most accessible food – liking them was no longer important. I'd hang around with my eye on the fridge till dinner time, hoping their mother would let me join them for their yummy-smelling meal.

'Isn't it time for you to go home now?'

But one mum in particular was nice. 'Eat, eat!' she said.

I grinned to myself between courses of cabbage and crispy potatoes, politely declining the roast chicken.

'I am now a vegetarian,' I explained. I had finally succumbed to full-time vegetarianism when I was sitting on a swing in Kensington Park chewing a takeaway chicken wing. *I'm tearing at the wing of a bird*, I thought. It didn't feel right.

I don't know if my friend's generous mum had any inkling of what I lacked at home. I never said anything and she never asked. But I think she must have guessed: my dress, too light for the time of year; my coat, absent from my skinny shoulders; my shoes, made of cheap canvas, scuffed and worn down. *I'll take a pair of Kicker boots in pink, if you're buying*. I loved Kicker boots. Shoppers queued in the Kings Road day and night for them. I wished I could join that queue. If they didn't have pink, I'd be going for blue.

I got my period for the first time after dinner in their house. All that blood, bit of a shock. And the pain. My friend showed me what to do. I thought I'd be older than 11. I didn't want to go back home to tell my mum. There was no point. *Mum, I don't want to be a big girl yet. I want to be a child for a little bit longer.*

I walked down to the huge red-brick estate and tried a fag for the first time with my cousin and his friends. I coughed and didn't like it. He thought me silly. At least I didn't pretend, carry on for fear of losing face. On my return I thought my mum might be angry when she smelt it on my breath, but instead she just cackled.

'You had to try it sometime, dear,' she said. She wasn't bothered by my shenanigans at all. *Mum, Why are you like this? Why have you changed?* I should have been pleased, I had nothing to rebel against.

Brown flares and Gucci shoes

'You're lucky lucky lucky that *man* is not here!' my mum spat, when she saw me looking at an old photo of my dad that I'd found in a shoebox. He was smiling in brown flares and Gucci shoes, leaning on a bronze Jag, the rich man's car of choice.

I looked a bit like him, with my wide smile. Apparently I acted like him too, cheeky, endearing. Maybe, but he had a tough Irish temper from losing his mammy so young. Cancer took her far too early. I guess he'd have not been quite so merciful about the ciggie I had just had.

My mum snatched the photo away. 'You can't miss what you've never, ever, *ever* had!' she said angrily.

Dad, why did you leave? My mum told me often that you wanted a boy. When I was born, apparently you wouldn't even look at me. I'm so sorry I wasn't a boy. I wanted to be one when I heard that's why you left. For a while I refused to wear dresses and I put on an old cowboy hat in the hope you would come back.

It's not fair! You could have taken me ice skating, there's a really good rink in Queensway. They do lessons there on Saturday mornings, but I wouldn't need them because I'd be going with you. Hungry afterwards, we could have walked to a workman's cafe and ordered orange- and brown-coloured food. Baked beans with mushrooms for me; sausages, bacon and hot buttered toast for you. With my tummy topped up you could have taken me to a funfair in Hyde Park. Then on to a rowing boat and splashed me with your ham-fisted rowing. And when I fell in from you tossing the boat a little too hard, you could have saved me from drowning.

You could have taught me how to swim.

Where are you? When bombs go off in London I wonder if you are near.

My mum has no money, but apparently you have plenty. Was it your idea to send me to private school?

Sometimes, on my birthday, a present appeared from you, ridiculous and over the top. One year it was a huge doll with a christening dress on. This year, a computer. It just blinked at me, I didn't know how to use it. Dad, you needed to show me how.

17 December 1983

A bomb detonated around the corner. That was the day you rocked up in your flash car, left the engine purring and your fur-coated girlfriend sulking while you ran up the stairs to see me. I wasn't there. You put 80p in 10p pieces in a neat little pile by my bed. No matter how much I needed that money, it remained there, unspent. The only tangible reminder I had of you.

Tyres and tin cans
December 1983

My mum was spending less and less time at Portobello market now. Sometimes she never went out at all. She'd run naked from room to room. Throw herself from wall to wall. Her body large, her body bouncing, sweat dripping from her flushed cheeks. On one day she halted abruptly. Her nose touched mine and her face contorted, snarling like a dog and gnashing her stained teeth, as she called me a, 'Fucking *who-o-rrrre*!' For 'flirting' with the dustmen.

But Mum, I wasn't even here on collection day.

With her matted pubic hair on show and dangly droopy breasts, her flesh wobbled while she mumbled to herself. She shook her head, found a coat and moved heavily towards the door. I waited – *one, two, three* seconds – and followed.

I saw her across the road. I backed away, hoping she hadn't seen me. There was so much anger in her screwed-up face, piggy-eyed and bright red. She walked briskly up the Embankment, stopping at crisp packets, cigarette ends, used tissues. She pulled a thin plastic bag out of her pocket and with precision, placed the rubbish in. When it was full, she brought out another, continuing till she was loaded up with four or five. Then she climbed over the railings and down the slimy stone steps to the bank of the River Thames. I watched, scared for her as she scavenged around, finding tyres and tin cans before the tide came in. Laughing excitably she ran for the nearest exit.

She had turned into an unpaid bin man, a bag lady. A blank stare, eyes glazed. Not normal, not there, not hearing me. She seemed mad. I did not want anyone know near this tramp of a woman with greasy wild hair, collecting waste while shouting profanities was my mother.

My many uncles and aunts couldn't see the problem when we met before Christmas for mince pies at the Troubadour.

'Ah, she's harmless,' they said.

You try being with her all day!

'So charismatic, so entertaining,' they continued, as we watched her prancing about between the tables wearing tinsel.

Yes, maybe for a minute, not your whole life. Never switching off, she's a nightmare!

'Stop fussing, she's perfectly acceptable.' Ignoring the fact that she had just knocked over someone's drink.

I was so frustrated, they had no idea. They'd look at their sister giggling like a toddler and say, 'Ahh, she's all right.' How did they know? They were never with us.

'At times your ma can be a great craic!'

Are we talking about the same woman here? She can't even sit still long enough to drink a cup of orange and cinnamon tea.

They were in denial. My blood boiled out of anger and defeat. I was not believed, but my mother's behaviour was *not* acceptable. They must have found her illness shameful, far too painful to face up to. They cooed their goodbyes and said, 'Love ya!' with no meaning. Then looked on amused while they watched me and their sister leaving with her nose in the air, as always, and today a Christmas paper hat on her head.

'Don't leave me!' I wanted to shout, knowing I had a miserable festive week ahead of me, but I didn't because my mother had taught me to believe, *Everything is fine*.

I was five years old the time we did Christmas properly. I stood wide-eyed by the big pine table watching as my mum peeled Brussels sprouts – mini cabbages I thought they were, hundreds of the bloody things – and threw them into a huge saucepan. Uncle Danny was there drinking Guinness while other rellies were spliffing up, and my little cousin from the 18th floor chewed on a Smarties tube. We sat next to each other in identical Aran sweaters, playing guessing games. With their bellies full and their heads high, my rellies sang rebel songs one by one in a circle, the others silent, respecting each new act. Crackers, party hats, laughter, hugs and sloppy kisses.

The next Christmas they didn't come.

Bread and beans
February 1984

I had no idea why my mother walked around with her nose always in the air, our circumstances certainly didn't warrant it. She replaced my shoes with ones far too big from a charity shop and my rain mac with a navy trench coat meant for a man not a girl.

'There is room to grow,' she said, pleased with her purchase. She didn't notice that I looked like a clown in a dead man's coat. And I didn't notice that I was beginning to look just like her. There was dirt ingrained in my neck, hair matted in dreadlocks, school skirt splattered with food and knickers reeking and no one noticed till it was commented on by Little Miss Alice Band, who had turned into a snobby little shit. 'You're a tramp!' she cried. 'A dirty smelly tramp!'

We had no hot water at home. My mum had let the bills pile up and the gas had been cut off. The only time I had a wash was when I went for a swim; I loved being clean. My hands were blue and my toes numb when I arrived back home in the cold. This was not clever as we had no heating either. We still had electricity for some reason, but no electric fires. As for light, there was just the one working light bulb, which followed us from room to room. I had to screw and unscrew that bulb 50 times before bed. At least the exercise kept me warm.

'Where's that bulb? I need it back. Give it to me *now*!' my mother screamed as she scrabbled in the dark for a candle then made her way to me in the bathroom where I was brushing my teeth. Shame we didn't have any matches. She felt her way forward like a mole, then, coming into the light, stepped on the side of the bath, reached up towards the bulb and fell over. Muttering to herself she tried again and again till she managed it. With mittens on she tentatively pushed up the bulb with her fingertips, turned it to the left and freed it from its bayonet fitting. Then bounced the bulb from hand to hand like a hot potato till she found her way back to the kitchen, climbed on to our pine table with the help of her elbows and in pitch black slotted it into place. That 100-watt shone. After its turbulent journey I was amazed it hadn't blown.

While looking for something my mum came across a mirror. She looked right up close at it and screamed. She head butted it, smashed it. 'He's going to get me-e-e-e-ee!' she shouted.

'Who, Mum? Who?' Then: 'No,' I repeated, for the hundredth time, 'no one is going to get you.'

There were more paranoid ramblings.

'You nasty horrible tart!'

'No, I am not nasty and horrible, I am your daughter.'

'Don't, don't cut up my clothes!'

'No, I am not cutting up your clothes. I am simply taking them to the launderette to wash them.'

No one is coming through your window.

No one is coming into your bed.

No, I am not telling you to kill yourself.

I poked through her purse and her pockets looking for spare cash as I couldn't collect her benefit till first thing Monday. Desperate, I burrowed in drawers, in cupboards, behind curtains, manically looking for 2ps, 5ps, 10ps, anything to buy a bit of food with.

'You little thief!'

'No, I am not stealing from you. I am going up the road to buy some bread and milk.'

'You're leaving me!'

'No, I am not leaving you.'

She thrust her fist in my face and screamed: 'Liar, liar, pants on *fi-i-re*!' Her spit landed on my chin.

I sniffed a gold can of hairspray and didn't come back for the whole weekend, staying out in some flat where all that was played was the Smiths and all that I ate was my own sick. Meanwhile my mum remained in a bed that smelt as if she'd pissed in it, not caring that I was up to no good, high from the hairspray and comatosed from Blue Nun. This was my life. I didn't think about it, I just accepted it and washed her sheets when I eventually got home.

On Monday morning the queue at the post office stretched ever longer, waiting for 9.30 a.m. and £19.65. There were old dears on widows' pensions, some frauds on disability allowance and the genuine on child benefit. I hopped from foot to foot, arms folded, listening to the small talk. There was a feeling of camaraderie as we all claimed together: no shame, just acceptance and impatience at the postmaster's slowness at opening his doors.

We tumbled in. In the shop section girls my own age were buying sweets and giggling. I longed to be them, to have their easy smiles. *Girls, I want your life; I have no chance just to play. I want your clothes; I squirm in charity shop finds. I want your innocence; I know far too much.*

I was so serious now, I'd forgotten how to laugh. I have become a carer to a crazy mother.

Broadsheets and shiny shoes
November 1984

I reluctantly agreed to accompany my mum to a craft fair near the Westway. On the Tube she hit her head hard with her fists. *Punch, punch, punch.* Commuters started moving away.

'Cunt! Cunt!' she cried at them. 'You fucking *cunt*!' My mum spat as she spoke. 'You stink. *Poo-ooo-wee!*' Her mood changed violently. She laughed hysterically while hopping like a flea from one seat to another. 'Look at your tie, your shit tie,' she shouted to one startled passenger. 'Aargh! Bad shoes,' she added, pointing at his feet. 'Baddy shoes, baddy two shoes,' she sang at the top of her voice. Suddenly she made a shrilling sound. 'Ahhh, ahhhh, ahhhhhhhhhh!'

A woman put her hand to her ears. *Don't do that, lady*, I thought. My mum crept towards her. With teeth clenched, she gave the women a vicious smile, then bent towards her ear. 'Ahhhhh!' she screamed, louder. 'Ahhhhhhhh!'

The train stopped. Terrified, the woman hurried off.

I suggested to my mum that we did also. I tried to usher her quietly off the train. But she had a sudden burst of energy, barged past me and ran down the platform screeching obscenities. I turned around for a moment. *Would no one help me?* But the commuters seemed too unsettled by the incident, looking down at their broadsheets and shiny shoes. They ignored me; I was invisible.

You're shaken, commuters, but what about me? I have to live with this every single day. No one wants to know. The rest of my family can't handle it, why do I have to? When did this start being my job? I am a child. Don't I have the right to be a child? I don't want this life. I feel guilty, commuters, guilty. Guilty for not wanting to look after my birth mother any more.

As I pushed through the train doors they closed sharply on my neck with a thud. *That hurt.* My head was stuck fast outside, my body helpless within. The train jolted, it started to move.

It is my time, God help me, it's my time.

The train juddered to a halt.

I am still here, I am meant to be.

The doors opened.

I am freed.

Commuters giggled nervously around me. I had wet myself. I couldn't stop myself from crying.

Is this how life is supposed to be? Please make it stop!

An adventure
December 1984

One, two, three, jump! Off the number 11 bus, down the Kings Road, past Chelsea Town Hall. I turned left into my street, doing my best to ignore the shouts and laughter of the middle-class children playing in the private garden square, up to my front door, hurrying because I needed the loo.

What's this?

A strange brown metal cover. Puzzled, I stepped back. *Am I at the right house?* Shock. *Yes, I am.* I felt a tightness in my chest.

A notice stuck to the door announced that we had been EVICTED.

I placed my hands on the metal casing, thinking, *If I push hard enough, it might open.* I shuffled from foot to foot. *I want to go into my home, walk through the door and use the loo, my loo. I want to say hello to my mum, even though I know I will not receive a reply. I want to go to the kitchen and try and find some food, even though I know there won't be any. I want to GET IN.*

With my fist in a ball, I banged on the metal. 'Let me in!' I cried. 'Let me in! I want my school bag that I left on the stairs this morning. Please, let me in!'

No tell-tale warning. No packing of boxes, furniture stacked precariously in the corner, no excited talk of a new home, a new beginning. Why had this happened? It was my fault. It was *those* letters, those unopened letters, piling up at the door that I had ignored and Mum had stepped over. I'd only ever opened one, a warning notice of unpaid rent. I should have done something.

Looking around, I saw that the street was empty. That was no surprise, it was always empty. It housed old ladies and well-to-do families. Their impeccably dressed children were brusquely ushered from car to kitchen, then back out again to that private garden square.

The air was crisp. I shivered, I only had my jumper on. My coat behind metal, my mother never ever nagged me to wear it. The light was fading, the street lamps flickered on. *What do I do?* I screamed in my head. *Where do I go? Where is my mum? I want my mum.*

I ran back up our street to the Kings Road. Finally I spotted her, twirling on the pavement in a filthy flowery dress. She was grinning wildly, surrounded by black plastic bin bags.

'We're going on an adventure!' she cried, dancing round and round, her loose hair slapping me with every turn.

'A holiday?' I asked hopefully.

She waved a grubby cheque in the air. Her tiny spidery writing had spelt out 'one hundred pounds'.

'Go cash it!' she ordered, flicking it out of her hand.

'Cash it where?' I asked, jumping up and grabbing it before it landed in a puddle. Studying it, I knew it would bounce. Her cheques always bounced. I tried to catch her eye. Pirouetting, she looked everywhere but at me.

'Mum, Mum, Mum!' I shouted.

'What an adventure!' she screamed back.

Hidden homeless

My mum and I arrived at a B&B in Earls Court with just the few things she'd brought in her bin bags. She had thrown me in some clothes and shoes, but forgotten my hairbrush and manky toothbrush. The room was on the third floor, tiny, with just a sink and two saggy beds. It had brown geometric wallpaper and walls so thin you could hear the rhythmic banging next door. There were strange moans from other rooms, too, but apart from someone playing Kate Bush, no high voices. I was the only child in the place. *How long will we be in this hole? Weeks? Months? Years? Will we get another flat? Will I ever get my belongings back?*

But the council had cleared the lot: my books, my school bag, my beloved Lego. I wouldn't have minded never again seeing that navy trench coat two sizes too big, or the Laura Ashley dress my mum had found somewhere, far too small. But the council never gave me a chance to say goodbye to my comfy bed, knitted pillows and old cuddly toys lined up in a row. My patchwork quilt – it meant a lot to me: the rainbow colours and the different fabrics, the smell, the familiarity. Why couldn't the council have had an Evicted Kids Toys Holding Room at their facility? Then losing my home would have been softened by not losing my teddies too.

Goodbye flat, goodbye.

We shared the only bathroom on our floor in the B&B with a creepy middle-aged man. There were dirt rings around the chipped blue bath and a sopping wet vinyl floor. *Where's the soap? The shampoo? The towel?* I quickly dried myself off with my school jumper, scared the crappy lock would fail, the door burst open, and the man would be standing there, staring right at me.

I raced back towards our claustrophobic room in just a T-shirt, now damp from my hair. The creep was in the corridor. I froze as he blocked me. He lowered his head to my ear and whispered, 'You're a budding page 3 girl.'

I darted out of his way, but his eyes longingly followed me. Heart pounding, I turned to my mum for reassurance. But she was lying in her own mess, mumbling, oblivious to me.

Mum, get up. I need you. She rolled on her side, clasped her fanny tight and yelled, 'My belly is full of yucky stuff!'

The next night I got my period. So much blood. I wanted my mum but she wasn't there. She had gone out and not returned. I wrapped her rotten jumper round me and curled up on her bed wishing I had a hot water bottle. My friend from school had one, I wonder if she'd lend it to me? But I don't have a kettle. Maybe I could borrow the B&B's.

In the morning, I dressed in my school uniform, which was filthy, as usual. I sponged it down as best as I could, grabbed some knickers that I'd rinsed out the night before and left on a warm pipe and hurriedly put them on. I tore off some toilet paper and stuffed it in my knickers as a makeshift sanitary pad. Then I tried to pull my tights on, with difficulty. They were so full of dried sweat they practically stood up on their own.

I must remember to rinse my cardboard tights tonight.

I combed my hair with my fingers and rinsed my teeth at the sink, wishing I had money for toothpaste.

BREAKFAST BETWEEN 7 A.M. AND 9 A.M., a sign said, pointing to the basement. The smell of fags hit me long before I entered the dank room full of a job lot of pine.

Threadbare tinsel hung on top of a gaudy mirror frame – a pathetic nod to Christmas, less than two weeks away.

The room was thick with smoke and hunched-up figures. Groups of forlorn men and one or two frail-looking women sitting silently. Were these the forgotten people? If they went missing, would anyone report it? If they died would anyone care? A funeral service would be unnecessary, as no one would attend.

My mum was not among them, I would have heard her cackling a mile off. No one looked up, as I squeezed through and sunk down beside a bay window with blacked-out glass. No one seemed concerned that this was not a good place for a young girl on her own. I was half expecting, 'Where's your mammy?' But no one seemed to care, apart from the creepy man drooling in the corner, scanning me. I knew what *he* wanted. And no one talked. I wanted bickering, laughter, at least the radio. All I heard was the sound of slurping, crunching, the click of a Zippo, the draw of a cigarette, the occasional turn of a tabloid and cars hooting on the Earls Court Road.

A small man with a sour face shuffled up and handed me soggy toast not quite browned enough. There was one measly portion of butter and another of gluey marmalade on a disposable paper plate. That was it, no Kellogg's variety box in sight.

I don't even like marmalade, I want my favourite jam, damson jam! I wanted to shout, but said nothing and just got on with munching. I was hungry, always bloody hungry. It was better than nothing. I was always a glass-half-full kind of kid. Besides, my next meal was not until my free lunch at the private Catholic girls' school my mother had insisted on sending me to. Normally we had packed lunches that we'd bring in ourselves, but when I'd failed to do this, the nuns started asking questions.

'And where's your lunch this time, Marni?'

'I've forgotten it again.'

'Is everything all right?'

'Yes, everything is fine.'

After five days on the trot of me nicking apples and breakfast bars from the other girls, the nuns took it upon themselves to feed me. They sat me separately from my friends in a large unloved room. I thought it a bit odd, but didn't complain when they gave me a cold medley of cheese, beetroot, coleslaw, iceberg lettuce and the like. *A bit bland,* I thought, but I was grateful. It was nice to use a knife and fork for a change, have a proper sit-down meal.

Now I hurriedly ate my toast and acknowledged the sour-faced man's services before leaving the B&B. Leery eyes followed me again, as I walked up the stairs and out into the open air. I took the Tube to school, the fare paid for by my friend again. Soon I was going to have to jump the barrier, or worse walk. I didn't think she could sub me for much longer.

When I arrived at the convent, the head nun ushered me into an unfamiliar dusty old room full of armchairs. 'You will not be returning in the New Year,' she told me. 'I'm afraid your mother has not paid the school fees. Her cheque has been returned, twice.' It couldn't have helped that my mother had called her a harlot at their last encounter.

Marni, I had a meeting with the nuns today. I'm afraid it's just not possible for Mummy to pay the school fees any more. I should never have sent you to a private school. Being a single mother on a part-time wage, I was wrong and I'm very, very sorry. Your dad said he'd help, but he didn't. I should have known. I will find a lovely new school for you to go to, and you can still see your old school friends.

Oh dear, I forgot, I didn't have that sort of fairy-tale life, with that kind of mother. Where did I go with my school uniform, now redundant? Some twelve days of Christmas this was turning out to be.

King's Cross Station
23 December 1984

Mum, Mum, where are you? Mum!

She had gone missing, I wished she'd come back. The last time I'd seen her was in bed at the B&B. I roamed the city alone, hopping on buses, avoiding fares, ending at her favourite station. She was bound to be here somewhere.

Can't you see me, commuters? The girl with blonde hair. I am the broken bundle not moving in the middle of the station. I am lost, I need to be found. I want a wash, a cuddle and a freshly baked chocolate croissant. I want my mum, my old life back.

I am surrounded by people with places to be, rushing past. I don't know where to go, how did I even get here? Where are you going? Can I go with you? Please don't make me go back to that B&B, it's pure misery. Can I go to your office and draw on scrap pieces of paper? Or to your home and quietly watch TV?

It's Christmas. I can't stand Christmas. I can't stand this emptiness I am feeling. I want a home, a family. Cornflakes and freshly squeezed orange with the juicy bits. I want the chaos before leaving for school in the morning. 'Where's my hairbrush?' I want to shout. 'My toothbrush? I can't find my toothbrush!' But I can't find anything because I have nothing. It has all gone.

Can I go to sleep and wake up in January? Christmas will be over then. Lack of presents, lunch, a family, none of it an issue any more. With a New Year ahead, surely my life can't get any worse?

Can't you feel my loneliness? Alone, I am vulnerable, crying out for help. Desperate for attention, for love to fill the void in my heart. I raise my hand to my chest. The misery hurting, penetrating my thin skin, consuming my frail body. I am ripe pickings, ready for an abuser to pounce.

On a street I saw a lad throw a takeaway into a bin. *Waste not, want not.* So I ate it. I picked off the half-eaten fish to finish the last of the greasy chips underneath. Sometimes

I wished I wasn't a vegetarian, I'd have definitely been less hungry.

The blubbering wreck had at last come back from 'an adventure', and was now chattering away endlessly under her covers in the corner.

'I can feel it in me,' my mother kept repeating. 'Get it out, get it out!'

On Christmas morning, the day was no different. There was no feeling of the festive season here. No Christmas tree, the smell of fresh pine needles a memory; they'd have been half price down the North End Road by now. No paper chains hanging up, gummed together excitably the night before. What about my stocking? A satsuma at the bottom, nuts in their shells, chocolate gold coins and a pair of stripy leggings. I didn't see that on the end of my sagging bed.

Crisis, if only I had known about you. Does your charity let children in for lunch? Or is it adults only? Do you, by any chance, offer a vegetarian option?

I walked the empty streets all day. London was so still, it was as if the whole city had fallen asleep apart from one or two people who said 'Hello'. Why? They would have ignored me the day before. Christmas is a time of good cheer and pleasantries, I can't believe crimes are carried out on this special day. Thieves must be like me, desperate. Bit older and braver maybe, couldn't have been any hungrier. Unable to knock on any friends' doors that day, I was buggered.

Crisis. Trouble is, you have to find us, the hidden homeless. Do you presume we will find you? Or do you search for us? Under bridges, in stations. You did not find me.

Boxing Day was much brighter. I sneaked into my friend's house and had roast potatoes with ketchup for lunch, with copious amounts of Quality Streets afterwards, and bubble and squeak for tea. My friend's mum had so many leftovers, she never minded me that day. She even let me stay the night.

We mucked about with my friend's stepfather before bedtime. He was ever so friendly and loved to mess. Tickles turned to wrestles on the floor. I nearly had a stepdad myself once, he was the only boyfriend my mum had. They walked by the river and only ever held hands. He hanged himself. Was it something she said? Probably, she could be quite cutting. She nearly had another when I was nine, but I ruined it by parading in front of the man in her 'monthly' underwear. Her tatty bra and grey knickers fell off my bony body. The shame, I'm surprised she didn't kill herself as well.

I was woken at 6 a.m. the next morning up by the sound of my friend's mum sobbing down the phone. Clambering out of my friend's bed, I stumbled into her stepfather's room to find him with his arm stretched out and his mouth gaping open. Had he called out before he died of a heart attack?

My friend's mum stayed in her pink nightgown all day. The police came, the ambulance men came, friends came, relatives came. Then there was the silence when the priest came. We squeezed around the dead man's bed to say the 'Our Father'.

To whom? He can't hear you!

I was told to stand at the end of the bed, right by his limp foot. I counted his toes to distract myself from his cracked soles. *This little piggy went to market. This little piggy stayed at home. This little piggy, yuck, could the priest please close his cloudy eyes? I'm hungry. I wonder if it would be rude to ask for a bit of cereal?*

St Saviour's
January 1985

The landlord at the B&B must have been a hard bastard preventing a schoolgirl from entering his premises.

'I haven't been paid!' he thundered. Business was business, I suppose. On the upside, there would be no more limp toast and weak tea. *Where will be my third place to live? Fourth? Fifth? Will we forever roam? So far, this is not that great an adventure.*

An angelic social worker floated into my life. She had creases round her eyes and a great big smile. Finally the system had noticed me. It was all new to me. *What exactly do you do? Do I really need you? Actually, I don't care. I just want someone to look after me.*

Susan sat me down in her office at the council and gave me orange squash and a pile of biscuits. I'd have preferred Coke and a Crunchie. *I'm a teenager not a toddler.* Then she rang around various organisations trying to find me a new home.

But my mum will be back soon.

'Let's look into you staying with your relatives,' she said, and worked her way through the uncles and aunts she could get hold of on the phone. 'None with room,' she said finally, disappointed. *Bollocks, an uncle has a spare room in his flat, I've seen it. My other uncle has a house. My aunt has two. Their guest bedrooms are not prepared, because they don't want me. I must be horrible.*

'We have found you a foster home in Oxford.'

'No way!' I said. 'Too far from all I know.'

'A correction centre for older kids?'

'You've got to be joking. I'm a nice girl from a convent school. They'll eat me alive.'

'It might not be easy but let's try and find you a children's home in the borough.'

'What? You mean like an orphanage?'

'They are not called that any more.'

'Would it cater for my needs? I'm a vegetarian, you know. They can't be giving me stew. No fish neither!'

'Yes, I think the home would have no problem handling a vegetarian teenager,' Susan said with a smile.

'What about central heating? Will it be warm?'

'Of course.'

She eventually found me one that took younger kids, a place where she said I wouldn't have to worry about being bullied. 'They'll take you as an exception,' she said, pleased.

I wondered why they'd take me, but readily agreed. Not that it was my decision, I'd be living there whether I liked it or not. I didn't know that at the time. Susan was trying to make me feel empowered by including me in a discussion I had no control over.

There were more telephone calls and meetings, this time to find me a new school.

'The girl is clever, a whole year ahead,' Susan said in a call to a state school principal. 'You have to meet her!' Good old private school, mine had been a hothouse pushing me. It had worked. Who wouldn't have wanted me? All sweetness and light with finishing-school manners. Susan could even hear the Ts in my words. A succinct sentence, a clear voice. Unusual in her line of work.

I looked into the principal's eyes and shook her hand, just as all fee-paying pupils do, drummed into you from the very first day of joining the elite.

'You will be a welcome addition,' she said. Had she created the place especially for me?

Must have been my big grin that drew her in. The deal was done and I was off to the Catholic girls' grammar in a few days' time.

I was curious about the next stage in my life, especially the home I was about to inhabit. 'An adventure!' my mum would have said. 'How exciting!' Food I can eat and warmth too. I had no fright or sorrow, my feelings numb from losing her.

We passed my old house, knocked down to create double the volume, and turned left into a mass of concrete. The home was bang in the middle of a huge housing estate. It was another world from the leafy streets I was used to. This refuge was not large, bright, pleasing to the eye, ring-fenced and full of trees. That's what I'd been expecting, like children's homes I'd seen on the TV. But this one was surrounded by deprivation, an almighty urban jungle. The poor looking down on the poorer. *Are you sure this is a place of safety? A bolthole free from harm?* Teenagers hung out of balconies and cussed as I walked with my nose in the air through endless rows of assisted housing to a block with bland windows, not my type of architecture at all. It was just like the rest of the estate, no announcement it held the most vulnerable.

A shadow flickered behind the swirly patterned glass. Laughter escaped through the letterbox. Susan allowed me to press the bell.

Thanks, but I am not two.

A dark figure grew larger, moving closer. The rush of heat hit me as a man opened the door and stood there, grinning. I smiled back politely and made eye contact.

'This is Matthew,' Susan said. 'He runs the home.'

'Hello,' said the man. 'I am very pleased to meet you.'

'I am pleased to meet you too,' I replied, holding out my hand. His eyes were dark and penetrating.

'Come in,' he said.

A child ran by, then another. We walked past an office into a vast living room with well-worn sofas, bean bags and an old teddy bear larger than any kid. There were a lot of children and they were everywhere. Playing, shouting, fighting, talking, all much younger than me. I couldn't hear the stereo playing over the noise of a game, ending with a book flying through the air, narrowly missing the huge colour TV, a contrast to the tiny black and white we'd had at home.

'While the others sort the boring paper work let's go up and I'll show you your room,' Matthew said enthusiastically. He put his arm on my shoulder to guide me the way.

We walked past toddlers' bedrooms, full of colourful toys scattered about; past kids' bedrooms, with clothes sprawled on the floor; past staff quarters, with a lock on the door; then along the corridor down to the end to mine.

'Here's your cosy bed,' Matthew said, patting the quilt. The room was north-facing and basic but had its very own sink, just like Little Miss Alice Band's.

'It's all very nice,' I said, smiling, ignoring the marks on the dirty cream walls of shoe scuffs, scribbles and fingerprints.

'You've got a really lovely smile,' Matthew replied, moving closer, fixing me with his dark shark eyes. He had very white teeth for an unhealthy-looking man. Hair that was high on his head, sallow cheeks and big feet.

I didn't know what to say apart from a polite, 'Thank you.'

Beddy byes

'I'm the head man here,' Matthew said, when Susan had left, 'and I've taken it upon myself to sort you out and get you looking shipshape because I like you.' He grinned. I needed this help; I was a bit of a mess. He was going to be my key worker, he told me. If I wanted anything, anything at all, I should ask him.

'Here, come sit beside me,' he said, sitting down on my bed.

I did as he asked. He moved up towards me and started brushing my hair. It was so matted it hurt too much to comb it. He ran his fingers through it, slowly and gently, finding the knots, cutting them out one by one.

'We're going to have to get you to the hairdresser's, or you'll end up looking like a witch,' he teased.

He delicately took my feet in his hands, slowly peeled off my dirty socks, and started to clip my long, in-growing toenails. As he worked on one foot, he rested the other between his legs. *All spongy*. He clipped away.

'It tickles,' I cried, pressing my foot hard into him. He was so nice.

He gave me a new toothbrush with strict instructions to brush my teeth twice a day. Then he told me to grin. He ran his thumb slowly from left to right along my gums.

'Open your mouth,' he said. He peered in. 'Your tongue is all furry.' Then: 'We're going to have to register you with a dentist.' I prayed I wouldn't need fillings.

He escorted me downstairs and ordered food for me from the cook. I fed greedily on cheesy pasta.

'It's like a hotel,' I said. It felt like freedom. No more nutty mother to look after, no more horrid B&B. Now I had central heating, I wasn't going to have to layer up to go to bed any more. A bath in a bathroom, clean dry towels, plenty of toilet paper and toothpaste. Luxury! *This place is a palace. I am safe tonight.*

I fell into bed in new pyjamas and clean sheets with a light on in the hall. 'For comfort,' Matthew said as he hung by the door. 'I'm just outside if you need me.'

I sunk my head in a soft pillow and listened to the new noises. A loo flushing, a distant clanging of pipes, a low hum of some industrial machine, a murmuring of voices, and Matthew tiptoeing away.

Mmm, that ten seconds before sleep, I'm all cosy.

The next morning he took me for a check-up at the doctor's. I was as embarrassed as any teenage girl would be. Then on for an assessment with psychiatrists at the hospital. There were two men, garishly lit. I was so frightened my knuckles went white from clasping the sides of the chair. Why did they need to see me?

'It's just a few questions,' said one, with a cool smile. He asked me to complete a bunch of words on a sheet. I tried hard to circle the right answers. I didn't want them to think me stupid.

'You're very lucid,' he said at the end of our session.

What does that mean?

The shoe shop was much more fun. Matthew sat right up close to me on a padded bench while a lady measured my feet. Then we looked at the shoes to make a choice.

'Not ones with buckles, no way!' I cried. But we still ended up buying a pair of boring, good-quality ones.

'They need to last,' said Matthew, squeezing my ankles.

Then on to an optician, to have my squinty eyes tested for the first time in ages. It was dark in the little room, the test specs heavy on my face. Matthew watched from the corner, he wasn't leaving me alone, even for a minute. I was allowed to choose pink metal frames, but the prescription glass was so thick my new glasses still looked like bottle tops. At least they weren't NHS specs. I could see so much better now.

In the shopping centre he bought me other essentials: socks, knickers, sanitary pads.

'Tampons are much nicer,' he said. 'I'll show you how to use them if you like.'

I squirmed.

'Only joking,' he grinned.

I did my best to smile. I didn't want to offend him. He was looking after me, helping me. But this was a bit embarrassing.

Matthew linked his arm into mine and bundled me into a bustling cafe and sat watching me as I ate the chocolate fudge cake he'd bought me.

'My favourite!' I gobbled it up, leaving crumbs at the corner of my mouth. He leant over and wiped them away with his fingers. I pulled back, giggling.

'You're so lucky you've got me,' he said. 'Because I'm the leader of the home. I can bend the rules you know.'

He let me go to Chelsea Girl and choose new tops, trousers, a jumper, a coat. I was excited, I was being given clothes from high street shops, not charity shops. New clothes, never worn by anyone else, all for me. It could have been my birthday. When Matthew hugged me, I happily hugged him back.

'See saw, Margery daw, Jacky shall have a new master,' Matthew sang after tea at the home. I rode his leg as he jiggled me around and around. Up and down, up and down. It was fun, though I felt a bit awkward. How old did he think I was? He sped up and I laughed. 'Jacky shall earn but a penny a day, because he can't work any faster!' Fits of giggles, my skirt was right up. Matthew was panting.

'All line up now,' he cried to the other, younger children. 'Which one's first for a hug?'

'Me, me, me!' cried the eager girls, jumping up and down.

Upstairs, once he'd tucked them all into bed, Matthew came into my room, smoothed my hair with his fingers, and hugged me 'Beddy byes'.

The relief of being saved from my old life made me euphoric. A few days later I came crashing down and wanted to go home to what I knew. I missed my mother. Where was she? Moody and miserable, moping, I cried, 'I want to get out of here!'

'You'll be fine. I'll look after you,' Matthew murmured.

He petted me like an animal. *Mum, Mum, this man is all over me.*

'Come and sit on me,' he said. 'I'll give you a cuddle.'

His hand clamped hard on to my inner thigh and squeezed. 'Come now,' he said, trying to make me giggle. Then, ever so gently: 'Do you want to suck my thumb?'

'I'm not a baby,' I said, shyly, through my tears. I sucked it anyway, for comfort. He told me that all the children did.

Soapsuds everywhere

9 January 1985

Matthew was so busy fawning over me he'd forgotten to buy me a uniform for my new school. So on my first day I went in my private school skirt and jumper, much smarter than theirs. I was instantly hated for this. I also confused the other kids by sounding posh but living in a children's home.

What hope did I ever have of fitting in? Of not being ridiculed and bullied? I wasn't posh; I was pure council. I just had the accent, from a school I should never have gone to. Nor was I rich, wearing an old uniform from a place that my mum could never afford.

At break, I found the second-hand uniform office, and got myself kitted out for the term ahead. Grey jumper and skirt, worn with a soft polo shirt. I sent the bill to the home. I had always been self-sufficient.

At lunch, a dinner lady pointed me to a different queue for my free school meal. The shame of it. I was already seen as a loser. I'd rather do without. Girls heckled me.

Yes, call me poor, a slag, an orphan. Call me Irish-four-eyes if you want. Yes, my mum is mental. And yes, that's right, nobody does love me.

A punch.

That hurt!

Water thrown in my face.

Go away!

So draining, these little bitches, with nothing else to do.

Why did I have to resort to their level in order to be accepted? With my accent dropped, my skirt altered and raised to the height of my crack, I punched back and finally they left me alone. I had bigger things to think about. My mum was missing. I didn't know if she was living under a bridge or drowned in a canal. I needed Blue Nun, Babycham, anything, to drink myself silly, forget my loss.

I tried to skip school. I wanted to go where I was wanted, to Matthew. Those girls just saw me as entertainment, he didn't. He saw me as special. He gave me loads of hugs and lots of attention. It was like he was flirting with me. I enjoyed it. I responded by flirting back.

I didn't much like how the home was decorated, though. My mum hadn't had much furniture in her flat, but at least she'd had taste. My bedroom at the children's home had an iron bed with a carpet, if you could call it that, more like a mat in a crap brown colour. Why not in pink or purple? My bedspread was pale yellow. Who on earth had thought that was a good idea? And why so plain? Why not with flowers? Hearts? Anything in bright colours?

Strip lighting, not good. No one wants fast-food restaurant lighting in their bedroom. The council have to get it sorted. *Couldn't you give my walls a fresh coat of paint? Couldn't I have a fake fur throw and a big heart cushion on my bed as well?* I just want my very own den, to be allowed to decorate my space to make it cosy. I want a nice night light in the shape of a bunny, please, preferably in white, as a red glow at night will remind me of scary movies. A few pieces of furniture would be useful too. I'd like a dressing table, a stool and some fairy lights to hang across a mirror. Tiny trinkets for my alien bedroom, I know it's a bit shallow, but it might make me feel better. I want to find little knick-knacks I can keep, ornaments I can hold on to, sweet things I can bring home to my mother. We don't have a proper home at the moment, but she is my home. I don't know where she is right now but she is always with me.

'Can I put up posters?'

'Yes, but only with Blu-Tack,' the social workers said.

Duran Duran? Spandau Ballet? Wham? Forget it. I am not excited by pop bands. I am excited by the smell of clean laundry and a man with shark eyes. How about a lock on my bedroom door, so I can get an uninterrupted night's sleep when I want to? The head of the home has started to visit.

One night a little girl was dragged away from her mother by social workers and the police right outside my bedroom window. She was brought inside but her sobs never stopped while Matthew undressed her, washed her and put her in pyjamas. Usually bath time made the children laugh, the way he mucked about with them, soapsuds everywhere. But not tonight. Eventually he calmed her and she fell to sleep exhausted. Outside her new bedroom, I looked through the crack in the door. She was lying on his lap, sucking his thumb. *My* thumb!

Later I asked Matthew why the little girl had come here, but he wouldn't tell me. 'That's confidential,' he said.

At first my heart went out to the other kids in the home. Some of them had such sadness in their eyes, I felt sorry for them. I'd read them a story, play musical chairs, do colouring-in. But after a while I found myself switching off. I couldn't cope with my own grief, let alone theirs. Stabbing themselves with a pencil 'just like Mummy's cigarette'. Rubbing themselves like a dog. Wetting themselves to get a beating because at least it was attention. I became immune to their tears.

I lay awake. What was that noise? Were those tears in the dead of night from missing their mum? Or something much worse? I turned down the sound in my head. I switched off to stay sane. My ears became deaf to the sobs surrounding me.

'Let's play mummies and daddies!' A girl took off her knickers and told me to lie back on my bed and open my legs. I was frozen by fascination. She pulled up my top and carefully placed her fanny on mine. She started humping. She was confident, I was stiff. It tickled, I giggled, she'd done it before. She humped some more, bashing away at my pubic bone. Now it hurt.

'This is what all daddies do,' she cried.

I know.

Special love

There must be a manual for paedophiles: either immediate sexual assault – or they're devious, calculating slow burners. The leader of the home was the latter, very clever. He made me like him, rely on him, need him, confide in him, trust him. Then want him, even though I didn't fancy him, an older man with halitosis. Step by step, he groomed me.

A cuddle, a long hug, a stroke, a massage. Lying in his arms, sucking his thumb; he really liked that, and I really liked his absolute attention. Then he rested his hand on my mound, nothing more. He just waited. And waited and waited, for nearly a whole year. He invested lots of time in me, because he knew I was his best yet. My body didn't want him to wait that long. I think he knew that too. By the time the year was up, my body was begging for him.

He gave me hugs when I was sad, told me jokes to cheer me up. He was so nice. He gave me little prezzies: a pencil, a notebook, a Care Bear key ring. We'd have a play fight, then another. He'd grab me, hold on to me for longer than he should. Then he grinned at me. I didn't mind; I melted.

He took me shopping more and more. He let me have whatever I wanted.

Sitting in the window at Pizza Express he fed me yummy hot slices of margherita with his hands. He was more like a friend than an adult. He always listened to me: about my missing mother, or being bullied at school, or just about a new top I liked the look of in Hennes. I wittered on like any teenage girl, but he seemed fascinated in *everything* I had to say. He gave me a piggyback as we strolled back together to the home. I pressed myself against him.

He always came to say goodnight to me in my bed. He had his little routine by now. He stroked my forehead, my hair, my neck, my stomach. Little by little his hands went further down.

I felt so lucky to have the head social worker personally looking after me. I loved it that he was the leader of the home. He could do whatever he liked. Come and go when he pleased. Take me out with no questions. His air of authority was a turn-on, his power a huge draw. I liked to see him bossing the other workers about. Telling them I could stay up late, come back late, go out for most of the night. *The buzz of being his favourite. He really likes me.*

Months went by of the same pattern. Making me completely relaxed, reassuring me. Then he'd take it a little further. He'd give me a shoulder massage, pull down my pyjama trousers so he could massage my lower back. Then he'd put his hand between my thighs, tickle them, going higher and higher, then stopping, gently stroking, resting his fingers between my legs, leaving them there, taking them away.

One night he undressed me completely. 'Let me see you naked,' he whispered.

I didn't mind because that's what he wanted. I pretended to be shy, but I wasn't really, not with him. He looked at me for a long time. Then he lay beside me on the bed.

He spooned me. I felt him swell. He gently bucked. I felt at ease. I wanted him to buck some more. I'd do anything for him. I was under his spell.

Long days would pass when he was off duty. I would yearn for his next visit. I'd rub myself without thinking. I could think of nothing else. Then he'd be up beside me on my bed again. His feather-like stroke tickling me. Tickle, tickle, tickle between my legs.

'That's nice,' I murmured, lying back, eyes closed. His fingers were ever so soft. 'I really like *that*,' I said with a start.

'I want to make you happy, happy inside,' he replied. 'Would you like that?'

Yes!

His hand went down to my pubic bone and beyond. I could hardly breathe. Gingerly, he touched me in a circling motion. I felt a strange sensation, that tingling again. That lovely tingling. I felt sort of wet. I parted my legs and rose instinctively. Encouraged him to carry on. His dark shark eyes glistened.

'Have you done this before?' he asked. *I think you know the answer, yes I have, and I want more.* 'I'm just going to go in a bit,' he said.

His middle finger slowly slipped in, as all the while he gazed at me, smiling. Then I heard his breath quicken. He tried to go in further, far too roughly.

'Ow!' I cried. I shut my legs tight.

He looked so disappointed that I had stopped him from entering. I so wanted to keep him happy.

I panicked. I plucked up the courage to grab clumsily at his trousers and feel his bulge. I didn't really know what I was doing, but I had to do something.

Don't go off me! I have nothing else.

'Let me see it!' I said, cockily.

'Don't worry, you will,' he whispered. 'You will.'

He turned me on my front and stroked my back. Long hard strokes, his yellowing nails scratching into me, gently. His hand went lower and lower. His fingers searched between my legs. I couldn't move, my heart was in my throat. I was tingling again. He stopped. I wanted more. I had a sudden urge to grab his fingers and make him carry on. I was shy and confused, wanting it but not.

'Ever been licked?' he asked. He rolled me back over, spread my legs and bent down. His head was right *there*. I was taken aback and felt awkward. He sensed that. 'Relax, go all floppy. I'm only going to put my tongue where my fingers have been. Mmm, just *here*,' he said, smelling me again. He gently started lapping. Sucking.

Oh my God! His excited slurpings made my body give in and open wider.

Mum, Mum, where are you, Mum? You are losing me to a man and I am beginning not to mind.

His next night shift took a long time to come. I thought I must do something that he'd like. Once again, his shark eyes feasted upon my naked body.

'Spread your legs,' he said.

'I can do better than that,' I replied. 'I can do a crab.' And before he could ask what a 'crab' was, I leant back and arched with my knees wide apart. He gasped. His mouth opened wide. He knelt down and ate me.

I was hooked. I had not felt this amazing since – ever. I wrote his name all over school with my pink fluffy pen. I drew endless love hearts on my teddy bear notepaper. I so wanted more of his 'special love', as he called it. I was tingling at the thought of that licking, that exquisite licking.

Strawberries and honey

December 1985

A while later he said, 'Come to my room tonight.'

Yes! I thought.

The staff quarters were the other end of the hall. I waited till it was late and I couldn't hear a sound, then I tiptoed *one, two, three, four, five, six, seven, eight, nine, ten, eleven, twelve, thirteen, fourteen, fifteen, sixteen, seventeen, eighteen, nineteen* steps and lightly tapped on Matthew's door. We giggled as he coaxed me in and locked it behind me.

He turned, his loveliness was gone. 'I am going to enjoy you,' he said,

He roughly pulled down my pyjama trousers and tore off my knickers. 'I've been waiting far too long!' he cried. He pushed me back on his single bed and I landed on a duvet cover the cleaners had taken off mine the week before. He opened my legs and threw them over his shoulders till I was practically upside down, and starting munching me like he hadn't had food for a week. He was a crazed animal, not knowing what to do first.

'Yuu-u-umm!' His tongue darted in and out, in and out, his mouth opening, his lips drinking.

I am not sure I like it like this. I was scared, confused, embarrassed.

His fingers entered hard inside me: one, two, three.

'Ow!' I cried.

'I am making you looser, so I can fit,' he said, unzipping his trousers.

Is this a game?

Turning me over, he raised me on to all fours, spat and started probing, probing, probing. *It* kept slipping. He tried again. I felt the tip go in a little bit.

'So-o-o tight,' he murmured. More spit. Further, further.

He then pulled me apart with his hands. More spit. It jarred, finally it slipped in.

'So-o-o go-o-ood!' he cried. But I was hurting.

The repetitive slapping of flesh. *I don't like the noise, I don't like the pain, I don't want to be here. There-is-always-a-child-worse-off-than-me.*

At last he got off and faced me. I could feel his eyes staring into my mine. He became passive, his touch became gentle again.

'It's okay,' he said. 'Did I hurt you?'

I was crying.

'I am so sorry, so sorry, I didn't mean to hurt you, Marni, but I wanted to show you how much I like you,' he said, hugging me. 'I like you a lot.'

I don't want you to like me that much, I thought for a second, my body rigid with pain.

He seemed upset, it was as if he could read my thoughts. He pretended to cry. I didn't understand. I wanted my mum. *Everything is fine.* I tried to smile through the pain. *He mustn't go off me.* He gave me a big bear hug and cuddled me, almost crushing me, for a long time, until my crying became a whisper.

Gently, very gently, he started fondling me again with his fingers. I was so tense, all I could think of was the pain. He held me too tight, telling me over and over he loved me, while sucking my nipples like they were strawberries. Constantly smiling at me, rubbing me down there again, faster.

'Relax,' he said. I was terrified. I didn't want to lose him. *I must make him happy.* But really I just wanted to go back to my own bed.

His dick was hard. He squeezed it and waved it in my face. Willies were horrible.

'This is what I've really been wanting you to suck,' he cried. 'Go on,' he coaxed. 'You already know how to suck, just suck it like my thumb.' He pushed the end of it between my lips, till my mouth opened and I took it.

'See? Isn't it easy?'

I couldn't reply. My mouth was full of ugliness.

I started gagging. He tutted. 'I should get someone else to teach you how,' he said, getting horny at the thought. He removed himself, slid down my body, and started lapping again.

'You taste like honey,' he said. 'Enjoy it like you usually do.' But I couldn't. I was stiff. I was sore. It was searing. *Am I bleeding?* I felt raw.

'Fuck, I want to put my dick in you so badly,' he said, manoeuvring himself back into place. 'Relax, take me all in! You want me to like you, don't you?' He rubbed the tip of his dick back and forth just inside my lips. I became swollen. Horrified, I felt turned on. *How can this be? The tingling, tingling. How can I feel this tingling when my fanny is on fire?*

He gently stroked my hair. Through the dim light I could see a kind expression on his face. 'Let go, baby,' he said. 'Let go!'

And, to the delight of the Leader of the Home, I came for the first time, sucking his thumb hard.

Dear Mum,

I wish I'd had a normal mother who took me up Oxford Street shopping, then got the bus home and cuddled me on the sofa in my dressing gown while letting me watch That's Life! *as a special treat. Who cooked me beans on toast, gave me the facts of life and took me to get my first bra.*

Why did you have to become ill when I was so young? Why not wait till I was old enough not to need you? Because it was my fault you became ill, that's why. You became ill because I stopped being a child and became a woman. You saw my budding breasts and fell to pieces. You thought of yourself at that age. By the words you mumble and the way you act, it's as if you too have been abused. When I hit puberty the fear of it happening to me too rose up in you. Your tightly closed box with horrific memories had been forced open by your own daughter's changing body. You could not look at me after that. I disgusted you. You called me a whore, a slag. I repelled you. It made me repel myself.

I couldn't even look in the mirror at my new breasts. I strapped them down, hoping they wouldn't continue to grow. Then I pulled that mirror off its chain and put it away. I wore those flowery Laura Ashley dresses I hated to make myself look younger, to please you. I sang, hopped and skipped in front of you, but all you did was push me away. You would not even make eye contact with me. You stopped kissing me, hugging me, smiling at me.

Then there were the voices telling you to hang yourself, throw yourself out of the bedroom window, kill me. You scared me. I started to look after you. I ran the household and opened the mail. Shame I ignored those red bills.

It was my fault you became ill, my fault we became homeless, my fault I am in a children's home. My fault I am a social worker's plaything. His name is Matthew, he's nice to me afterwards, but I can't tell you about it, I think you'll disown me. It would confirm what you thought of me – a whore. I want to be back with you in Battersea Park or on the beach in Brighton. But you're right, I'll never be that child again, for I am now a whore.

It was my fault, my fault I was abused. The very thing you did not want to happen, happened to me. If only you had been ill years later, you could have saved me. And now all I want to see is you plait your stupid hair.

Children in Need

Matthew gave me a five-pack of pants for Christmas, to replace the ones he'd ripped the week before. *That was generous of him*, I thought, *it was only one pair.*

I was given lots of presents at the home. *I wonder what Matthew gave his wife and daughter?* I thought. I got an electric toothbrush donated by Boots that must have been worth a bit. Stationery from Smith's; gloves and a scarf from Marks'; chocolates and sweets given by so many high street shops. On Christmas night, surrounded by parcels, with Matthew placing my humming new toothbrush on my fanny, telling me I was in for a treat, I realised that I was one of those Children in Need.

Dear Children in Need,

Where were you, Wogan, when I was being raped?

You were wittering away on the TV. Couldn't you hear me?

How do you get on to that show? I'd have thought a girl in care like me would have got front-row seats; with my thick glasses and cheap clothes smiling at the camera; so nice, so vulnerable, so sad.

I was one of those kids, a child in need, but I didn't see anyone coming to my rescue.

'Our mission is to make a positive change to the lives of disadvantaged children and young people right here in the UK.'

You missed me!

I was unwanted by my aunts and uncles. I thought blood was thicker than water. I was wrong. *I am an inconvenience, unloved by my family.* Only one wanted me, an aunt who tried in vain. But with only a studio flat, she was not allowed.

Dear Rellies,
I am told I'm a delight by a man called Matthew. He gives me lots of love, but he isn't even family. How nice of him to want me. He likes to come in my throat. With my mouth well versed, I guess I don't need you now.

The good life
March 1986

Children's charities seem to collect so much money from people on the street. A picture of a kid with pleading eyes on a 'Save the Children' tin is so much more appealing than a picture of a man with a mad glare on a 'Help the Mental' tin.

There was money for anything I wanted to do in the children's home. I got to go on a school ski trip, a day on a yacht and a weekend in France, to boost my serotonin levels. All because I was a child in need.

Hot dogs, thin chips and mayo served lukewarm in a picturesque square. *Yuck. I'll not be eating that.* Sausages do not pass my lips unless I am giving Matthew a blow job, even then I have issues about swallowing. *How can eating live sperm possibly be vegetarian? I'm a traitor to my cause.*

'J'ai voooudrais ketchup?' I stuttered. The waiter answered in English, always a bad sign.

After our meal, Matthew and I left the others playing pool and headed back for a 'special hug' in the boys' dorm. How did they not suspect? Matthew was salivating when I got up from the table and said, 'Au revoir.'

The hotel was not bad for the equivalent of a two star. Matthew had bought new tight white briefs for the occasion. Like I cared.

'What did you buy for me?'

Black suspenders from a boutique, in extra small. Selfishly, they were really for him. But I still said, 'Merci.'

I feasted on the foreign chocolate he'd bought me, while he munched on my minge, ignoring him till he hit the spot. Then I raised my hips and let him have me.

I was all sweet smiles and innocent looks back in the girls' dorm. I was lying there on the bed reading *Just Seventeen* when the others came back, smirking and smelling of chocolate, with my new suspenders hidden under the sheets.

In a way I was rich. Going on excursions paid for by the state. Fun activities comped by charities. Freebies from unidentified companies. I liked it and I never wanted it to stop. Matthew sensed that. He knew that if he gave me a taste of the good life, it would be hard for me to resist.

Mr and Mrs Smith

Matthew gave me a gold watch from H. Samuel. H. Samuel! I never thought I'd get anything like that, ever. There were benefits to playing up to his demands. With every wank I got a prezzy of my own choosing, with every fuck, another. All I'd ever wanted was a *Blue Peter* badge, now I was getting a pair of 9-carat gold earrings from the Argos catalogue instead. 'Can I have some shoes from Dolcis?' I panted, as I raised my knees to my chin. 'A top from Chelsea Girl?' I cried, as I pulled at his hair. 'A Filofax with all the bits in?' I said, spreading as wide as I could. I then crouched over him and bucked in his face the way he liked it.

He spent ages down there. Fiddling, staring, moaning. I looked out of the window and started to drift off, thinking of other things. My mother. *Where are you? Will we ever live together again?*

Eventually I'd hear a muffled, 'Keep fucking my face and you can have whatever you want.'

I became used to finding this middle-aged man molesting me upon waking. Slipping silently into me, trying to kiss me, his bad breath putting me off. But it was worth it for all the affection, and now the prezzies.

'Can I have this bracelet? On page 242, this one?' I asked him, in my best baby voice when I was in his room, fucking him. He removed his dick and shoved it straight in my mouth, without even wiping it on the sheet first.

'Oh yes!' he said with his wide grin. I retched, he tasted disgusting. I tried pushing him away. 'If you want the bracelet,' he said, 'you have to pay for it.'

I wanted to learn about sex, I had to get better. Besides, I liked having a purpose. I didn't want him to go to anyone else, anyone younger. *At least I know what's going on*, I thought. *I can handle him. Someone smaller might end up mad, like my mother. He wouldn't, would he?*

My demands became larger. A £20 trinket, not a £10 one. I was learning how to be a whore without even knowing it.

Matthew needed somewhere else to take me. The staff quarters were too close and even though he seemed to get off on the thrill of being caught in my room, it had to be short visits. In and out. No noise. Quick relief. Just in case. If he didn't silence me with his penis in my mouth, he silenced me with his hand as he fucked me. But he was getting frustrated. He wanted longer, he wanted more, and he wanted me to scream.

I enjoyed the desire that Matthew had for me, the moment he admired the view. He took me out after school and fucked me there and then, wherever. Bus stops, parks, cinemas, a train. *Fuck-fuck-fuck*. Buying a bus ticket when he was up me, what a kick. How did the conductor not notice? Must have thought he saw a daughter on Daddy's lap. But he was stroking me. I was surprised he didn't report us to Social Services.

Being banged hard in the toilets of a fast-food joint while eating my hot apple pie. Matthew rolled a five-pound note and shoved it up my fanny while I busily sucked out the gooey apple.

'You can keep the money if you go back to school like that.' He grinned that wicked grin of his.

'Easy,' I replied with a forced smile. It was not. Must be what an oyster feels like with a pearl inside its shell – irritating.

On his next shift, Matthew crept into my room. Aroused, he held my jaw and raped my mouth. He withdrew and replaced his penis with a cubic zirconia ring.

'I've been wanting that,' I gurgled.

'Manners,' he said. 'Where are your manners? Now hurry up and say thank you, I want to get out of here.' Then he bit me. On my neck, my shoulder, all over. I was confused. I was used to all this sexual abuse now and I liked it.

I am disgusting.

His mess in my hair made it all knotty the next morning. I combed it, long painful strokes. The silence of loneliness was interrupted by my faint whimpers. I wanted to hurt myself. Then I smiled.

Such a naughty big bad secret I've got,
Giving me naughty bad gifts.
There's a naughty big bad man in my bed,
Telling me to do naughty big bad things!

Matthew drove me up the A40 in his battered yellow Ford Capri and stopped at a sleazy motel. They must have known we were no Mr and Mrs Smith as we checked in, but they never said anything. Up in the privacy of a dingy en suite, he upped the ante.

'Piss on me!' he demanded. He plonked his arse on the toilet and beckoned me on to his lap. I unwillingly wrapped my legs round him. Face to face, I looked down and saw my lips wide open, with his dick twitching, aching to glide in.

I was feeling awkward, my wee wouldn't come out.

'I can't,' I said, all shy with my sideways smile, instinctively covering my mouth.

He leant over and ran a tap, then tickled me all over. When that didn't work, he lay in the bath.

'Straddle me,' he said.

'I don't want to,' I replied, full of attitude until my glasses steamed up. Then I was insecure. He pulled them off and threw them into a corner. I need my glasses to find my glasses, he was well aware of that. Without them, I had to do as he said.

He flung out the soap rack. I knelt there in the bath for an age with the water running and him waiting. He slid down and licked me, then lathered me. At last my wee came. A fierce flow, quite yellow, popping the bubbles and staining the foam. I was giggling, he was gasping. *It* was up. He got hold of me, positioned me and shoved it right in.

'Ow!'

'I' – thrust – 'like' – thrust – 'that!' he panted, and with another thrust he shuddered, bashing my knee on the enamel. With his eyes closed, a grin spread across his face.

'That was good,' he said.

No, it was not. But I must keep pleasing you, for fear you will go off me.

Back at the home I insisted I had contact lenses. 'I am old enough and responsible enough and they're as cheap as glasses anyway,' I argued to the staff. They finally agreed. The tiny pieces of plastic gave me so much confidence. Once I'd learned to place them on my eyeballs without poking myself, I could lip read all the time. I didn't want to take them out at night, they were my armour.

I stirred from sleep to find the lenses stuck fast. Blinking furiously, I pinched my eyes with my fingers to prise the contacts from my cornea. I dropped them into saline, my saviour, a solution that not only cleaned, but made me free. Free from the fear of my glasses falling off, free from the panic of not finding them, free from the world of not hearing. At last.

Jaw ache

I started to get the odd invite home from girls in my class at school. Surprising, seeing as I was the one everyone looked down on. But a quiet girl with no mates asked me to come back to her flat after school. Better No Mates than no one, I thought.

Her mum took one look at me and hurriedly put away her jewellery. She watched me suspiciously. I lounged on her sofa leafing through an old *Vogue*. She wasn't rich, she must have nicked it from the doctor's.

'I want a house like that one day,' I said, pointing to a fine, double-fronted dwelling on the back pages.

'Why do you dream of the impossible? Your ideas are way above your station,' she sneered. She squeezed herself into her tiny kitchen to make us some tea, darting in and out every two minutes to make sure I wasn't misbehaving.

I much prefer my mum to you, I thought wistfully.

Her daughter went in to help her. 'What did you bring that little whore home for?' I heard her say. That hurt. *I'm not a bad person, I've just had bad luck*, I thought.

She practically searched my pockets as I left.

'Would you like to come to mine next week?' I asked my friend.

'Okay,' she replied.

We slipped past the barriers at the Tube station and walked to the children's home, taking turns listening to Depeche Mode on her Walkman. When we arrived at the estate I ignored the cries of 'There goes the unwanted!', 'Nobody loves you!' and 'Slapper, slapper, slapper!'

My friend looked pensive. 'Do they ever stop staring?'

'Don't worry,' I told her, 'I'm used to it. They're quite tame today. Usually it's, "Your dad is a murderer and your mum is dead!"'

I made eye contact and said a polite hello to Matthew in the office. There were kids in every corner as usual. We stepped over a cleaner and blinked as we walked into the harsh strip lighting of the kitchen and grabbed a load of shortbread.

Up the stairs we went, past closed discoloured curtains hiding us from the outside world, then along the corridor to mine.

'So private,' my friend said.

'Yes,' I replied. *It's the perfect place to be abused.*

'Wow!' she went on. 'It's like you're rich or something. Cooks, cleaners, all these people to look after you, all you're missing is a mum nagging you. You're so lucky.'

She sat on my bed smiling, the same bed I had fucked Matthew in. She moved on to my chair chattering, the same chair I had sucked Matthew in. She slid to the rug laughing, the same rug I had...

I couldn't concentrate, suddenly there was too much in my head. I had to get her out.

We met Matthew on the stairs, smiling sweetly. His groin bucked hard into my arse as I passed.

Get off me!

That night Matthew could not get it up. To arouse him I bent double. Nothing. I slipped down, not even a twitch. Frustrated, he lay with his flaccid member in my mouth, just in case. I got jaw ache.

Next morning before school, he tried me again. Limp. Was he feeling guilty?

Matthew went to the doctor, who raised an eyebrow when he said he was seeing someone young.

'I didn't tell him how young,' Matthew giggled. 'But he was rather taken aback,' he went on. 'Anyway, you're not that young.' *Why didn't Matthew's doctor tell? Why can't I?*

'Everything is fine,' I'd say to anyone who asked. The words my mum had taught me to say by rote.

Everything is fine.

Officials

I was half hoping someone would find out. Catch Matthew in my room, or me in his. But I was so scared of the consequences, the embarrassment of it all. I had no family to talk to. I couldn't run home to my mum and cry. Or whisper to my dad: 'There's a bad man telling me to do *things*.' But even that wasn't true, because I was doing *things* to the bad man as well. How else would I get a pair of Adidas trainers? Matthew was so clever, giving me the presents I wanted.

How could this abuse go on for months and months and no one notice? No one see me tired, bunking off?

No one see how Matthew behaved around me? Now he was staying at the children's home even when he was off duty. 'I'm having marriage trouble,' he told the other social workers. 'Me and my wife need a few days apart.' And they all felt sorry for him while he was upstairs molesting me.

'Put me in your mouth and fall asleep,' he told me. 'That's it. Use me like a dummy. Suck me while I stroke your hair.' He fingered me instead.

I had a doctor, a social worker and a counsellor. The words were right there in my mouth. Wanting to spill, scream, shout at the top of my voice: 'I AM BEING ABUSED BY A MAN WHO'S PAID TO LOOK AFTER ME!'

But I could not be heard, because nothing came out. I beat myself up wondering why I could not tell.

All those officials held a meeting about my situation, how they'd handle my case. 'We will take steps to eventually rehouse you with your mother when she is well again,' they told me. There was an oppressive feeling of pity in the room. Half a dozen adults sitting around a table, smiling at me. Matthew was among them, he looked just like them; but the others hadn't violated me the evening before. Matthew's eyes were not wrinkling, his smile was not real.

Why couldn't I tell that nice plump lady on my left that the child in me had died a few months before? Why couldn't I tell that non-threatening-looking man on my right what had happened only last night? Why couldn't I tell my angelic social worker, Susan, who had led me here a year ago: 'I have a tissue down my knickers because I am bleeding come.' Feelings of shame immobilised my mouth, feelings of fear stopped me from coming forward.

I looked over at Matthew. 'It's your fault,' he would say if I blurted something out. 'You wanted it. You asked for it, you came to my room.' And the officials sitting around that table would agree with him.

'Yes, you went to him of your own accord. You are the one to blame. Because you like it.'

Pocket full of posies

My mum had been found gibbering, under a bridge. She had been sectioned and locked up on a mental health ward. Deemed a danger to herself or others.

I hopped on the 31 bus and rode on the top deck to an understated building in Chelsea to see her.

'She has a chemical imbalance of the brain,' a psychiatrist told me when they realised I was her daughter, 'possibly from a severe knock to the head or a very serious childhood trauma.'

They had diagnosed her with schizophrenia. I felt relief that her illness had a name, then overwhelming grief for the loss of the mother I'd never had. Resentment that I'd had to cope with this alone for all these miserable years.

I saw my lovely mum across the ward. She smiled drunkenly at me, trying desperately to open her eyelids wider. Her head was so heavy, she couldn't even get up to greet me. From serious mess to serene mass. What a shock.

She gave me a necklace with my name on it, and a sailor's outfit meant for a 12-year-old. 'It looks quite large,' she whispered hopefully. *Mum, I'd forgotten you don't want me to grow up.*

It was boiling on the ward and she was ever so sleepy. I was claustrophobic, I had to get out. Looking at her body, lying there, so pathetic in a hospital nightgown with her hair everywhere, I wished she'd die. Wouldn't that be kinder? Couldn't I assist her? She gave me the impression she wanted to go. But killing is illegal. I gave her a kiss on the forehead instead and said goodbye. I was in tears that night. I crept along the corridor to see Matthew. 'All I wanted to do was brush her hair,' I cried.

'Suckle me,' he replied. 'It will soothe you.' He was right. I lay for an age sucking him, without thinking. Very reassuring. Then I got a cuddle, which turned into a fiddle, finally a fuck. I wasn't in the mood for that.

'But I am on.'

'Great! We can play our game,' Matthew said, in a frenzy. He loved it when I had my period. Just the aroma made him tumescent. He turned me on my side and, lubricated by my blood, he glided in easily.

'Pretend I stabbed you,' he said eagerly.

I lay there motionless.

'All this blood,' he murmured excitedly. It turned him on to think he was fucking a corpse.

He came prematurely. He didn't withdraw, determined to stay in me till he could go again.

But he slithered out.

I worried I wasn't the only one Matthew wanted. Among the younger ones, there was one in particular that he liked. She had large, almond-shaped eyes, a turned-up nose, auburn hair in ringlets, dimples in her cheeks. She was always on his knee jiggling, jiggling, jiggling, while he sang, 'Ring-a-ring o' roses, a pocket full of posies.' I knew that game, that game had been played on me. *Hope she goes home before she is ripe, as he is ready.*

Bounce. She landed on his groin and carried on jiggling and laughing. It seemed Matthew had forgotten where he was. Then he caught my eye. I felt sick.

Not her, she's too young. Me.

Flustered, he shooed her away and rushed to the loo. I followed him into staff quarters, to finish him off.

'Let me in! Let me in!' I cried.

He opened the toilet door and grabbed me. I flicked my knickers to the side and pushed my fanny to his face. His eyes dilated. As he pulled me apart, he came. I was relieved. *At least it was me.*

'Practise holding in your wee, it will keep your fanny tight,' he told me. Alarmed, I did as he asked. I had to keep him interested, I must not be replaced. 'Soon I'm going to show you how to shave till you're smooth,' he said.

Like her.

Blue note

Matthew got turned on by the thrill of fingering me in public while I ignored him. Even if I'd wanted to, I couldn't respond as I was busily doing my homework at the home's kitchen table while other staff chatted to him, oblivious. All I could do was surreptitiously open wider as he whispered, 'I have to be with you all night!'

So I pretended I was staying with my quiet friend. When the other social workers on duty were about to check, Matthew said, 'Don't worry, I know where she'll be, she's cleared it with me.'

I packed my toothbrush and we sped off. We checked into a B&B in Earls Court. *Not Earls Court!* At least it wasn't the same one that my mother and I had stayed at. The men at reception ignored my age and my school tie. The majestic building, its high ceilings and intricate cornicing, had been ruined, elegant windows severed in two. Soft beds were draped in seventies colours, curtains in swirls. The carpet was thick with dust.

I sneezed.

'West End Girls' played on the radio. I leant back and arched with my knees apart, while Matthew performed cunnilingus.

'Move your hips like a whore, little girl,' he said. Then: 'I want you to rub yourself all over my face.' I changed positions. Then he rammed a Twix right up me, hard until it melted. Chocolate poured out of me.

'Just like blood,' he exclaimed, smearing the gunge all over his face. He popped Maltesers in, one by one, sucking them out in a frenzy. Melted to mush, the crunch from them gone. His mouth like a wound when he surfaced. *Ugh!*

'On all fours!' he commanded. Now he tried a Mars, gently easing it in. 'Go with it,' he told me. I pushed back and held my muscles tight, to stop it from oozing. It was uncomfortable, hard to keep in. *Yuck!*

He nibbled, sucked, bit, till only the very end was left inside me.

'Release!' he cried. It slid into his mouth. When he'd finished, he plunged his tongue in me to prep me for my 'rape'. It hurt less if I completely relaxed. 'Rape-rape-rape!' he cried, as he slammed into me.

I was immune to the word, he said it so much. He wanted me to say it too. 'Say it. Say it!' he shouted.

'I don't really like chocolate, you know, up me,' I said afterwards.

'Oh dear,' Matthew mocked. 'My poor baby. This will help.' He threw a five-pound note on to the dark sticky patch on the bed. I picked it up between thumb and forefinger. That gooey fiver gave me a surge of excitement I only otherwise felt when his tongue was teasing me. A blue note was better than any present.

'Now say it!'

'Rape-rape-rape.'

The men at reception sniggered as we left the next day. I pulled up my skirt and flashed my chafed patch at them. It was red-raw. They were not laughing now, I saw.

Once a prozzy always a prozzy. After he'd given me money, there was no going back. Was it the same for him? He told me that once he'd tasted fresh meat, it was hard to return to his wife.

Placing my hand on his packet in the car I said, 'I'll do anything for more money.' He grinned that grin of his even wider and got a boner at the thought.

Heavy traffic

Matthew picked me up from school and drove fast to his dilapidated house on a dual carriageway.

Bad position, bad taste. Why did you buy this? I wanted to say. 'Quaint' was all I could muster.

With the flimsy door closed firmly behind us, he brought out an alcopop from a plastic bag. My favourite was vodka, mixed with anything. It had no taste, which suited me.

'My wife is out,' he said, as I drank and he dragged me upstairs to the marital bedroom.

I looked into another life. An unmade bed drowned the room, a wall of mirrors made it bigger. An unfinished cigarette, cold tea and specs beside a thriller trilogy.

The smell of lavender from an open drawer, someone else's knickers. On a bedside table, photos of family faces I didn't want to know the names of. A cat meowing constantly, wondering who had replaced its owner.

He kicked his wife's cat out and said, 'I want you bare.' He led me to his out-dated bathroom, where he showed me how to shave. With every strip that he scraped, I screamed, thinking it would hurt more than it did. My cries a huge turn-on, my fresh spots of blood too tempting. His thumb entered me roughly. Laughing, he promised to go easier on me next time. 'I like you hairless,' he said. *Am I not young enough?* I thought. I had to finish my drink.

Matthew could wait no longer. 'On the bed!' he demanded. Sinking into tipsiness, I splayed my legs wide in front of the mirrors. He told me to rise up and frig myself, giving me a little help on the way. But I couldn't, his kid's eyes were staring right at me. I turned away from the photos. He knelt behind me and clumsily plunged.

'Watch my cock slide in and out,' he said. I looked in the mirror. I didn't mind watching his dick, but I didn't want to look at my face, I don't know why. I thought of money.

'I need you so much tighter,' he said. He withdrew, pulled my cheeks apart, spat, then poked the other hole.

With my body in position and my skin so soft, it was there for the taking, my crevice so inviting. I screamed.

'No one is going to hear you,' he said. His torso bent over, he held my hand tight.

'Don't fight it, don't fight it,' he repeated. I saw me underneath a monster in the mirror. I closed my eyes and listened to the heavy traffic.

There's always a child worse off than me.

I arrived back at the home to find I had passed every one of my exams. Not bad for a girl who was rapidly becoming a drunk.

> *Throw me to the dogs, rip me apart, I'm a fucking*
> *   arsehole.*
> *Throw me to the devil, impale me, I need to fucking*
> *   die!*

Why do kids cry for their mothers, wives cry for their husbands, dogs cry for their owners, victims cry for their attackers, when they have been abused? Fear and loyalty.

> *Dear Court of Law,*
>   *Is this 'statutory rape'? Yes, I am just under age,*
> *but I'm also consenting, begging Matthew to touch*
> *me. I provoke him, beckon him into my hole for*
> *money. That's not rape, that's prostitution. Arrest*
> *me, not him. He's no rapist, he's my punter. Don't*
> *you dare take him from me!*

I missed him so badly when I didn't see him the next day. I called him at home on the pay phone, risking his wife picking up. He calmed me down with words that meant nothing. Then said, 'Go play with a banana, a small one, mind.' It wasn't as good as him, it went all mushy. Such a waste. The cook must have wondered why she ran out so quickly.

I cried when I didn't see Matthew on Day Two. *Matthew, if I had you now I'd beg you to go deeper.* 'You didn't call me back,' I howled, when I finally got to see him on Day Three. I made him fuck me over and over. He bought me a dummy. 'For the days you don't have my dick,' he said.

I'll do anything to make you happy.

When does grooming become acceptable? Become love? I now loved my rapist, my paedophile lover. I was obsessed with him now. I came while sucking my dummy, dreaming of him giving me a baby.

Snuff

'On top!' demanded the punter. The whore reluctantly mounted him. Grinding and groaning like a robot. A hooded man crept up behind her with a large axe, so heavy he needed both hands to hold it. She was too engrossed to notice. The punter's eyes widened, real fear. Bound and helpless he started screaming, a high-pitched screaming. The hooded man lifted up the axe, and in one powerful swing, cut off her head. Falling heavily to the floor, it rolled out of view.

This can't be a 15! I thought.

Her body carried on moving for just a second, then slumped, and lay there twitching, her blood pumping and spurting on to the hysterical punter.

The hooded man started hacking, cutting off the punter's feet first, then expertly severing his arms; the limbless body bucking, rising, as in orgasm. Only when the hooded man started on the victim's face, did the screaming finally stop.

Matthew came loudly when the punter's face finally fell off. That was his favourite scene: he played it over and over. He couldn't get enough of me sitting on his lap with my back to him, bouncing me up and down in front of his TV. He held the remote with one hand, frantically fast forwarding, rewinding and pausing, while pushing my body into place with the other. Sometimes leaning me slightly to the left to get a better view, all the while making sure he didn't pop out of me.

'I'd like to make a film like that,' Matthew told me with a grin. 'It's real life, you know.'

Life skills

The patient on the school television screen looked bloody miserable. With her legs parted, a see-through tube had been inserted. I couldn't see quite where because there was a white sheet protecting her modesty.

'Miss,' I asked, 'is that thing entering her vagina?'

The stifled giggles of the classroom turned to silence in nervous anticipation of what was to happen next. Bloody fascinating. Staring at the TV, we heard the patient's whimpers and the sound of a vacuum, *Scclluccbhssscch*. Then we saw the see-through tube filling up with her flesh and blood, spilling over into a plastic bucket. A no-nonsense nurse sifted through the waste with tweezers and placed a perfectly formed hand on a Petri dish. Five little fingers stretched out, a dead baby's hand. It looked like a doll's hand.

'It's not real, it's not real!' I cried to the other girls.

With her arms folded the teacher nodded as if to say, 'Yes it is'. She grinned while we screamed. The video was supposed to put us off abortion. What did we expect from a life skills class run by nuns?

Life skills, I had no life skills. I learnt most of them in the wrong order, by mistake, or by myself, but mostly from Matthew. Why wasn't the life skills class about refraining from having sex? Not that it would have made a difference. I didn't have a choice.

Suburbia

After doing a double shift, Matthew picked me up from school and we drove all the way to the suburbs with my feet on the dashboard and his hand between my legs frigging me to J. J. Cale. We finally arrived in his driveway after a quick tug around the corner. The man certainly liked to take risks. He had smelly fingers as he embraced his wife. Knowing I'd had Matthew's first load of the day, I bellowed a confident, 'All right?'

His wife was slight, blonde and pretty like a doll. She was doting towards her husband, amiable enough towards me, but also slightly wary it seemed. Their only kid stood watching the three of us. The girl was a carbon copy of her mother. She climbed on to her daddy's lap and sang with him before tea.

'Dada, will you marry me?'

No, he won't, and that's my bloody knee, so get off.

'I'm just going to use the loo,' I said, trotting up the stairs without asking for directions.

His wife went into the kitchen to prepare the tea. She was old-fashioned, Matthew was encouraged to stay out. I giggled with him in their front room while we waited. We sat on the velour sofa that had seen better days, with our thighs touching, my skirt high, deliberately trying to provoke him. He crossed his legs and stared at the TV that we had watched porn on only the week before. I noticed the beige carpet where his spunk had soaked right in.

'There it is,' I teased, elbowing him. It looked like yogurt. *Hadn't she spotted it?* He did that big grin of his.

Wispy wifey brought out buttered baps, cheese in foil triangles, sliced beetroot, coleslaw, iceberg lettuce, every type of dressing with clogged tops. I had to admit she'd made an effort. Then there was a bowl of cubed fruit salad, synthetic cream in a can, Victoria sponge 'made with homemade jam'.

'Damson?' I asked hopefully.

'Strawberry,' she replied flatly.

Bourbons in a tin, builder's tea in a pot. Wow, just as well her guest was not the Queen.

'Can I help you?' I asked politely, following her into the kitchen, pulling out some paper napkins from a drawer she thought I'd never been in before.

'That was a lucky guess,' she chirped. We sat down with Matthew at the head of the table.

'Will you have some tea?' she asked. 'Milk first or…?'

'I like the tea first, but that's not the proper way, is it?' I replied, giggling. Her eyes were on me, she was suspicious, wondering what my motives were.

I made a messy sandwich, dug in and smirked at Matthew, as salad cream dribbled down my face. A week before it had been his spunk, in this very room.

'Nice dress,' I said to the dutiful wife. 'Fancy a chocolate finger?' she then asked, and looked confused when I burst out laughing.

Matthew got a good ride on the way back home. And next time we went there, I made him fuck me in that crappy dress of hers. We got blood on it, my blood. Afterwards he had a panic attack. 'Oh no!' he cried.

'Oh dear,' I said, stifling my giggles as he shoved the soiled garment into a sink full of water.

'I'll say I spilt tea on it,' he mumbled.

'She'll think you were wearing it,' I replied.

I hope the fucking colour runs.

White socks and Vaseline

'Want to see where I came from?'

Not really.

'Okay.'

It was not up for discussion, Matthew made up his mind to take me there anyway. We drove to his childhood home on an endless estate in no-man's-land. His mother was away and his old room a shrine to her boy. It was all bed and no space and Matthew couldn't wait to get started. He wanted me lying on his manky mattress, wearing nothing but white socks and Vaseline. Freshly shaved and glistening, waiting for him to take my supposed virginity. I'd brushed my hair and braided it into two plaits, just as he liked it.

'Here, let me pull out your snake,' I squealed.

'Pretend you don't want me,' he said. I pulled in my new-found muscles really tight and acted unwilling, which turned him on even more. I had no choice but to let him in. I became subservient.

'Now suck your dummy,' he said. As I did so, I heard an ecstatic sigh. 'My little baby,' he murmured, pushing deeper. 'I must stop. I want to keep you tiny.'

'No, Dada, no, break me!' I cried. He loved that girlish, high-pitched cry, repeated over and over, with the words he'd asked for. I struggled, as he wanted me to, and his balls *slapped, slapped, slapped*. As they always did. My fanny farted in time to his grunting. A long low animal groan and it was over. Withdrawal, rest and money. Lots of lovely money.

Games were a great leveller, I almost felt equal to him. I dozed off.

I woke with a heaviness in my chest, a throbbing between my legs, a sadness that I did not understand, in a bed that was not my own. Then the games began again.

He drove me to a huge graveyard and ran off.

'Where are you?' I screamed, frightened in the dusk among the stones.

He jumped out and grappled me to the ground. Aroused by my fear, he rubbed himself frantically by a little girl's grave, laughing as he read out the epitaph on the upright stone.

Precious are the memories of our darling little daughter...

He scoured around for another grave to lie on in the moonlight.

An angel lies buried here.

'This one!' he cried, pointing to a baby's pillow-top gravestone. '*This is the promise, the life everlasting,*' he croaked, reading the curled inscription.

As a police car patrolled he pulsated within me.

When he drove me back, he stopped short of the home and made me walk the rest of the way. I tried to sneak in, but it was late, the door was closed. The social workers on duty accused me of drinking. I ignored them, had a shower and sloped off to bed.

Fumbler

'Wake up. You're going to be late for school!'

I had bags under my eyes, was very bad tempered, and couldn't concentrate in class. The teachers felt sorry for me, blaming my mood on the trauma of my having lost everything.

'I wished I lived in a children's home,' said my quiet friend. 'You have so many nice things,' she went on when we compared watches. *But I had to fuck hard for this watch, what did you do to get yours? Cuddle up to your mum?*

She and the other girls at school were excited when they got a pretty dress; I was excited when I got money. They were into teenage films; I was into porn. I was moving away from them. They seemed so childish with their stickers and posters of pop stars.

Quiet girl, go pop your cherry and we can be friends again.

Meanwhile, I flirted with any man I could find. At school, in the offy, the chippy, on the Tube. I pulled up my school skirt and wore no knickers, hoping they would be tempted to slip their index finger into my slit, moistened with their spit. Couldn't they twig that I wanted them to touch me so I'd have some power over them? I tried to get closer and closer to where they were standing, my skirt riding higher and higher. Should I risk grabbing their hand and making them touch me? Then I could tell on them and ruin them.

Good men got hot under the collar when I was around, dirty men got lucky with a grope, with me egging them on. *More, more, more!* I was constantly dripping. If Matthew couldn't get it up, I'd insert my electric toothbrush, courtesy of Boots the Chemist. I didn't mind which end as long as the batteries worked. I wanted to be messed with all the time and I was not even of age.

Upper form boys on the bus were skinny wastes of space. Spotty and greasy with a single sprouting hair, trying-too-hard hairstyles, overpowering deodorant and badly ironed shirts. But they were cocky, surrounding me for a feel on the crowded train home. I didn't resist, any one would do. I pushed towards them, goading them on.

Going back home with the boldest, I opened my crack and the poor mite came in two seconds. How was I suppose to compose myself? I thought I'd pretend to be innocent. Bit better, but bloody boring. 'Rape me!' I was dying to say. But I realised he had to learn how to fuck first.

He was so shit at foreplay, kneading my tits like they were dough. I bent over and raised my arse, so he could see my lips protruding, just as Matthew loved. He stood there staring. He didn't have a clue where to put his finger or his tongue, if he even dared.

'Come and make your finger smelly,' I told him. 'Here, let me show you,' I beckoned, then snatched his hand. He was petrified; I thought it funny. His mouth dropped when his finger came into contact.

'It doesn't bite,' I said.

I lay back on the bed and gaped myself open.

'Come on, have a good look now, that's it. While you're down there, why don't you have a lick? Come on, taste me. I know, let me sit on your face.'

That didn't go so well, too much too soon. I was loving his humiliation. I finished him off with a blow job so perfect he nearly fainted with the pleasure. I so wanted to straddle him, but we got caught by his mum. She was shocked, he was mortified, and I was laughing, refusing to get off. The poor boy was only going to realise how good I was when he went with another girl, a fumbler like himself.

It was better sticking to Matthew, with his pot belly that hung lower than his penis.

Now I had new demands.

'Piss on me, fucking piss on me!' I ordered. I had gained a lot of confidence.

He pulled out of his favourite orifice and I waited. Nothing. 'Come on!' I said impatiently.

'All right,' he replied crossly. 'It's almost impossible to piss with a hard on!'

Four seconds later, I felt the warmth of his urine on my back, rolling under my body, in-between my legs.

It turned me on. I demanded more.

'Shit on me, shit in my mouth,' I said, sniggering.

'That's disgusting,' he cried.

'I'm only joking,' I laughed. The tables were turning. Matthew didn't turn me into this disgusting child whore. I did. It was my fault. I had been the one who skipped into his bedroom that first night we did it properly in the home.

It was all my fault.

TWO

'If a woman approaches any beast and lies with it, you shall kill the woman and the beast; they shall be put to death, their blood is upon them.'

LEVITICUS 20:16

Cosy mattress
May 1986

'Not happy with being pregnant?' The adverts were
plastered all over the Tube escalator. I rode up and down,
up and down, three bloody times, trying to take in that
telephone number.

The clinic was on Tottenham Court Road. The
entrance anonymous. I mounted a flight of well-trodden
stairs and entered a dreary-looking room. I had been
impregnated and no way did I want it. A silly little girl's
fantasy turned into reality was not a dream come true.

The do-gooder staff clucked around me. I liked this
attention. They arranged for me to go to a local hospital
and have a scan to determine how old the foetus was. If
it was under eight weeks, I could have an abortion pill.
What, no op? Nice one!

Off I trotted. More attention. They squirted cold gel
on my tummy, turned the screen away from my sight line
and quietly assessed the situation.

'Can I see?' I asked, fascinated.

The radiographer looked at me with loathing. 'I don't think that would be appropriate under the circumstances,' she said. 'Do you?'

Appropriate? Was it appropriate to be fucked by a man old enough to be my father? Was it appropriate for him not to use protection when shooting his load? Was it appropriate for me to find out the age of my baby, when I was going to kill it in a few days? Appropriate that the radiographer looked at me like I was scum, when I was really the victim?

Don't look at me like that! I'll get someone to rape you, shall I? Bitch. Don't anyone look at me like that. I taught myself to swim!

But I liked an adventure, a new experience. I was off to have this abortion pill. Looking forward to the concerned nurse's face, the holding of my hand, ginger biscuits and endless cups of tea. Might ask for chocolate ones if I'm feeling cheeky. I felt bad for the baby, of course, and for myself, but I should be a realist, it didn't look like I was ever going to make it to heaven anyway, not with my track record. God was not going to take in a lapsed Catholic whore. My actions warranted a place in hell. What did I care? I didn't believe in that religious shit any more anyway.

What was the point in me attending Mass, eating a tasteless wafer they called 'the body of Christ', drinking red wine from a cup that had everyone else's spittle in that they called 'the blood of Christ'? The saliva of the congregation, more like. What was the point of dressing up in a white virginal dress with pretty flowers on and draping a veil over my rarely brushed hair for my First Communion? With my hymen already ripped, I hadn't even been pure then. And a few years later, what was the point of wearing a smart white suit to my Confirmation, when my mouth had already lost its virginity and my fanny had followed not long after.

What has God ever done for me? How can I believe there is a God when He is not looking after His children? When He is letting me be a blow-up doll for the devil himself. God has not entered me, God has not chosen me, God has not noticed me – a paedophile has.

At Family Mass on a Sunday morning I always said my prayers when I was asked to by the priest. I recited, 'Our Father who art in heaven, hallowed be thy name. Thy kingdom come, Thy will be done, on earth as it is in heaven. Give us this day our daily bread, and forgive us our trespasses, as we forgive those who trespass against us, and lead us not into temptation, but deliver us from evil. Amen.' In monotone, when I was kneeling down on those hard stools full of horsehair. I bowed my head, did not giggle and concentrated hard on what the priest had to say. 'Love thy enemy, he is your brother, he is your sister, he is your mother.' I gave out hymnbooks and sang my little heart out. 'Amazing grace, How sweet the sound, That saved a wretch like me.' I helped with the collections and did not take a penny out. Even though I knew there wouldn't be much in the way of food till school meals on Monday. I did all that, God, and You did not come when I needed you. All I could hear were the groans of a bad man on top of me. In-and-out, in-and-out, his sweat trickling down my body.

I thought of you, God, and prayed. 'You will be here in a minute, won't You, God? And this man will look at my pathetic body, break down and get off me. He will sob, say sorry and remove himself from me. Scoop me up, wrap me in a blanky, and deliver me from evil. Take me away and place me in the arms of a loving caring family, who'll wash me, dress me, and help me start again.'

But God, You never came. He came, came within me. Matthew made that fucking baby, and I am going to kill it.

I almost ran to the hospital on the allotted day of murder and entered a room full of morose-looking women sitting on institutional chairs. I found a place to perch and started flicking through the pages of some dog-eared magazine. I think it had been left for us 'slappers' to take our minds off the brutal killings we were about to commit. I was getting bad vibes from the other slags who were squirming in their seats. They *were* slags or slappers, weren't they? If I was a slag for letting men in, weren't they too?

I was definitely the youngest. I bet they thought I was at least 16. The nurse asked my name. 'Would it be Mary now?' she enquired sarcastically. 'Yeah, the Virgin Mary,' I retorted. *Call me whatever you like, as long as it's not 'whore'. Only I am allowed to use that word.*

I gave her a false identity.

The mums-not-to-be all seemed so awkward, avoiding looking into each other's eyes. Perhaps it was because they knew we were all there for one thing: those pills, the flush, the end. A new beginning, start again as premeditated murderers.

There were 12 of us miseries sitting there. If I included those unsuspecting babies in the womb, that was 24 of us in total. Maybe one of these hosts was carrying twins. Christ, maybe I was. That meant there could be as many as 26 people in the room! Bollocks to babies not being viable until 24 weeks. If its heart is pumping, it's a baby to me. 'Babies in the room, babies in the bin. Blossoming babies, bloodless babies,' I sang to myself not so quietly.

A bit stuffy in here. Boring. How long do I have to wait?

For a room full of women it was unnaturally quiet, apart from the faint screams of nearly new mothers wafting in from an opened window. Maybe the nurses thought that we'd hear them and change our minds. Not likely, by the sound of it giving birth was torture. That would have been all of us before the year was out.

'Cheer up!' I wanted to say to the would-be killers. 'Life and death, one in, one out, that's what it's all about.' But I'm sure I'd have got a whacking, so I said nothing. I always said nothing. I never said anything about anything.

Who'd listen? I have no voice.

At last! The sympathetic face of a nurse came along.

'Now you do realise, that once you have taken this pill, it will terminate the foetus.'

Foetus, don't you mean a baby with eyes, a heartbeat, and a couple of buds for arms?

'Yes, I understand,' I said, all grown-up. 'But can I have a cup of tea with this pill instead of plain old water? Two sugars, please.' Why did the wanker of a nurse give me the same look as the radiographer had last week? I thought she was in the caring profession?

'To expel the foetus,' she went on crisply, 'you have to come back and take a second pill the day after tomorrow.' Why was she treating me like a child? *Because I am one.*

I'm not stupid, maybe a tad skewed by certain events, but not stupid. Why can't she give me the second pill now, so I don't have to bunk off school again? Does she not trust me to take it? Will the baby lie dead in me for weeks, rotting, poisoning my body? Gripping me with fever, making me ill and die, if I don't come back? Will the baby only be half dead and slowly dying, if I don't return to finish it off?

Why don't they invent one pill instead of two? That would be so much easier and cheaper. These medical scientists are quite clever, surely they can just keep practising on mice until they crack it? Then they can trial it on messed-up, angry young girls like me, who will take anything, in any orifice, for the right amount of money?

The grim reaper handed me the pill and without hesitation, I swallowed. She walked around the stuffy room and gave it to all of her ladies in waiting. *Slurp, swallow,* silence. *Slurp, cough, swallow,* silence. *Slurp, swallow, sob,* silence. Right, we're back down to 12 people in the room again. Unless there's a little fighter in one of their tummies clinging on to life.

I left.

Do I feel any different? I thought as I lay in my bed alone that night. The answer was no, and I went to sleep. I woke up to my bed vibrating. My T-shirt was up and Matthew was wanking. He licked his long fingers and shoved them right in. 'I need to suckle,' I said; then: 'Pray, pray with me.'

I recited the 'Hail Mary' and convulsed. A comfort. I had come praying many times before.

I chose not to tell him about the abortion. *He'll want that baby. So he can fuck it.*

Two days later, at the killing department at the hospital, I took the second tablet, 'Yeah yeah yeah,' I said, listening to the information about what would happen in the next few hours. *Bor-ing!*

I wore a soft pad and waited for the baby to arrive on its cosy mattress. Cramp, blood, bits, clots. I saw no baby. Where is it? Did I miss it? Did it not come out in one piece? Where are the five little fingers? A dead baby's hand? I was disappointed not to see its black beady eyes, say 'Byeee' and flush it down the loo. I was hungry for Maccy D's.

My darling baby,

Sorry baby, up, up in the fluffy white clouds. Sorry for the life you never had, the tears you'll never shed. Your first tooth, first steps, first jump. Your laugh, your joy, your wonderment at the world. Your first piece of mashed up banana. Your first feel of the rain, the first time you see the snow, enjoy Christmas. I had to kill you, please forgive me.

That baby haunted me. I tried to fight thoughts of it out of my head. But babies and pictures of babies were everywhere. When that baby crawled into my head, I would throw it out. But it kept crawling back, right back in, it was alive. It had gone from living in my tummy to being in my head, feeding on my brain. I punched myself to get it out. 'Get out, get out, go away and leave me alone!' It then grew bigger and ate all of me. I was now that baby, that baby had taken over me. The only way to get rid of it was to run in front of a bus in Kensington High Street.

Bang! All I got was a serious bruise on the right side of my head and a bad headache. Not death as I'd hoped, the bus wasn't travelling fast enough.

'You okay?' said the driver, leaning out of the window. He didn't even get out of his cab.

I decided to research suicide and kill myself properly. I could hang, gas or electrocute myself. Slit my wrists, drink bleach, fall off a cliff or a bridge, whichever was closer. Jump in front of a Tube train, eat talcum

MARNI MULHOLLAND | 113

powder, what did that do? Or down alcohol and pills. But what if my suicide attempt didn't work? What if I only burned my arms off? Or blinded myself? Or just ended up paralysed?

Did I really want to die? Go to nothing? Because I knew there was no heaven. I'd be a dog that died in the gutter, nothing more. A carcass. My skin only clothing, barely covering my soul, lost from within. I only have one life. *Don't die yet, not yet!*

I did not want to go to sleep, I was starting to get nightmares. Drowning in harrowing thoughts of suicide and death repeating over and over. I knew I was dreaming, but I was stuck in semi-consciousness and couldn't get out.

Wake up, wake up, it's time to wake up now. Please, brain, allow my body to wake up!

I was screaming but no one could hear me. I was asleep.

Panic attacks, crying, trembling. I didn't even want to have sex. I wanted this shit to stop, because this wasn't right, this was not how life was supposed to be, this was not how *I* was supposed to be. Why was I telling a paedophile I loved him? Why was I always having to reassure him? I don't want to be warped, to desire an old man. I want to meet a boy, fall in love and have natural and healthy sex, whatever that is. Will it ever happen? I want to start all over again, be reborn. But am I too damaged? I want to find the strength to become normal. Have a normal, happy life.

The gift
July 1986

I was back to square one, living with my mad mother. Somehow I'd convinced the dour officials in my yearly review that she was stable enough for me to live with her. How had I pulled that off? Surely that was not my decision? It was certainly cheaper to get rid of me. They rehoused us round the corner from the home in a hard-to-let council flat.

With a cold tiled floor, we had Charity Allowance furniture and a Freemans catalogue, tempting me with new clothes for a minimum monthly payment. But nothing had changed: the lack of food, the filth, the howling. My mum was mumbling to herself as usual, trying to scrub off I don't know what from decades before.

I tried to stop seeing Matthew, but he knew how to tempt me back in. Money. I was living in the poshest borough in London where it seemed cash was everywhere apart from in my pocket. Others had it, why couldn't I? Boys with stripy shirts and girls with pearls were larging it up in Golf convertibles, cruising down the Kings Road in the sunshine. Matthew was well aware how pathetic my life was. Friday night and all I had was a few coppers for food until Monday, the poor man's day of pay.

He found our flat and parked outside it for hours on end, with 'Slave to Love' blaring out, hoping the song made him seem more attractive. *It will take more than the dulcet tones of Bryan Ferry to entice me.*

Later that night he buzzed on the intercom. 'I have a gift for you,' he said. *I wonder if it's a stereo from Dixons? I will be tempted but I must refuse.*

'Go away!' I shouted. He waited an age until a neighbour entered the building. Then he caught the closing door and boldly stomped up the 28 steps to our flat, knowing my mum wouldn't even notice his presence. He banged on the chipped blue door until I couldn't bear the noise any more. Then he came in and sat on my bed, picking out my dirty knickers from the laundry basket and smelling them, until I agreed to go with him in the car for a tenner. He'd lied about a gift, the gift was the tenner. He knew how hard it was for me to say no to a fee.

'It's the last time,' I said.

I slid into the passenger seat. Matthew shoved my head down. A lorry drove by, as he adjusted the car seat and lay back.

'Do you want to play daddies with me?' he asked. *Not really.* But I did what was bid for another tenner.

'You may not have a gift for me,' I said, 'but I have one for you.'

He gasped when I pulled up my skirt and he saw my hairless 'gift'.

'Daddy, do you want to stroke me, there? Feel how smooth I am. That feels so nice! Shall I open wider? Oh Daddy, I like that very much. Daddy's going to make me come with his hairy bear hands! Oh Da-da-da-da! Now stretch me so I can sit on you. Let me bounce up and down on your big thing. Fuck me, dear Daddy, please, fuck my tight little gift. Pull me open! Wider. That's it, ease yourself in. That's it! Is that good? Am I being good? A good little girl for you? Now let me feel your come, dear Daddy. Oh Daddy!

'This is the last time,' I said, as he came in me on my 16th birthday.

Annoyed by the finality in my voice, he shoved me off him and sped away fast. I had no time to put my seat belt on.

'Slow down!' I shouted, scared shitless.

He laughed and drove till the car shook, weaving in and out of traffic on the Westway, with Clapton strumming on the tinny radio. I begged him to, 'Stop! Stop! STOP!'

Finally he stopped, called me 'boring', threw me out and drove off, leaving me past Perivale in the pitch black.

I walked for miles in the rain, soaked through as I didn't have a jacket. My shit shoes hurting me, so cheap and ill-fitting. I jumped into a prowling car with an offer in broken English of warmth and a lift. No warning signal went off in my teenage head as I sat beside a man whose build was way too big for his car. My instincts had died long ago.

I was hardly surprised when he parked up in a quiet backstreet, walked round to my side and got in. He positioned me below him. I felt his weight. I didn't protest. I lay there lifeless, thinking of my bed waiting. I didn't even retch from his rancid smell. He seemed disappointed when I didn't bother to react to his heavy thrusts; confused as I calmly pulled down my skirt when it was over and said nothing when he dropped me off in Shepherds Bush. *I am so used to this, so numb, so over it. What's another man anyway? Does it matter? I have no respect for my body, it no longer feels like my own any more.*

Day's wages
October 1986

I became a Saturday shop assistant in Chelsea for crap money. I had the charm and the smile but not the right clothes. So I was given a crisp shirt to wear with a full skirt and told to brush my long blonde hair. My uniform allowance didn't extend to shoes. Disappointing, as I thought I'd be able to choose a pair from the current collection. I couldn't even steal some, the owner's eyes were glued to me.

'You have a very dirty look in your eye,' he purred.

I know.

I hated not having shoes like the girls who lived in private garden squares, so I soon swapped my wages for navy leather loafers, to the delight of my new boss. But I was back to where I started from, no bloody money. That didn't last long.

I wasn't shocked at how readily I agreed to let him have a feel of me for cash. I liked his schoolboy excitement on asking, his breathlessness before he touched, his ecstasy on making contact. Nor was I surprised when he suggested he go further and stick it in me. I said yes, of course. He didn't ask the other Saturday girl, though. Mind you, she was minging.

A night with an unknown would make no difference, I thought. I'd done it before. I knew what to do; be willing and very vocal. Like girls in porn films, just as Matthew had taught me. I'd get it over with quickly. Besides, the owner wasn't a complete unknown. I was almost looking forward to it. But I wasn't expecting his friend as well.

I felt so self-conscious. Out of my comfort zone. In my head I liked the idea of a threesome, but I didn't want it when it was for real. I froze, told the owner I had changed my mind, but he ignored me. He had to undress me. Naked, I tried to hide under the covers. But he pulled them off me, uncurled me and reassured me, holding my hand while his friend forced me open and entered me. The owner was gentle, stroking my hair while his friend gained rhythm.

'I don't want to,' I whispered, with a tear running down my cheek.

'Just look at me,' he replied.

When his friend was done he settled me, but he still had to have his turn. He had a hard-on from weeks of anticipation. Urgently he mounted me. He was big, it hurt, I was sobbing now.

He gasped. *I want to be back with Matthew,* I thought.

Two men were scary but the money was good. I wasn't, lying there stiff as a board. I certainly didn't deserve a day's wages. I was neither willing nor vocal. The owner didn't ask me to do that with his friend again.

'Next time just you and me,' he said.

I felt shit. I jacked in the Saturday job. I had another career now.

One more night

Just one more night, which I knew would lead to another, then another. I passed girls in Alice bands and boys with floppy hair as I disappeared into basements with men in cheap suits. I made it clear I came with a price. They laughed and fucked me anyway. Being pumped yet again with a blank stare, I vowed I wouldn't do it again. But Matthew had started all this. *Where is he?* Money was becoming ugly to me.

Just one more night. I needed a drink.

'Come here!' Yet another lowlife pushed me into a mouldy bathroom and parted my legs. Liking what he saw, he unzipped his flies, took out his penis and pulled back his foreskin. It wasn't purple, it was dog-cock red. I'd seen this one before. My head was pulled in for a closer look of his grotesque member before it disappeared into my mouth. Then, nicely lubricated, shoved into my hired hole.

He was on top, crushing me. *I can't breathe.* My bare body on the floor, an unflushed toilet by my head. *The smell.* My hair, wet from patches of piss under the toilet bowl. Couldn't he at least drag me to the carpeted floor of the bedroom? Why all this urgency? One glimpse of my labia and they're all in me like a shot, no thought for me. Why rip at my skirt? Men are so selfish.

Just one more night. They think I'm young, younger than 16, that's why they like me. Let them think what they like, I don't care, I get more money this way, I'm a rarity.

The power I had when I said those three words: 'I am illegal.' All men were paedophiles to me. Not one declined my offering, only coming quicker in my loins at the forbidden thought. I must have put on my old school uniform more times than when I was actually at school, white pants being requested the most. I pulled them up tight so they could see my camel toe.

'No, to the side, I want to see your slit,' said one. 'Now pretend to resist, rise. Let me in.'

I clamped my muscles tight.

'No, no, no!' I cried, wrestling with him, before I released. So mindlessly boring, not much imagination going on here. Change the record. Why always a schoolgirl? Will I still be doing this routine at 18? 30?

Do all men really want to fuck a schoolgirl? Are all of them aroused when driving around in their saloons? Clocking girls in pleated skirts, tight shirts and ties askew, skipping home? What is stopping half the nation from getting out of their cars and grabbing them? Hundreds of men, raping them all in a row. The fear of jail, nothing else. Do they think about those girls when they shag their sagging wives? Imagining a schoolgirl's tightness while they're pummelling a scraggy fanny. *Paedophiles!*

Is this life really any different from being with Matthew? Sitting on the faces of men much older than me, who get off on me for the same reasons as the Leader of the Home?

Yes. Because it was different, I was older, I was in control. This time I was not forced to have sex, I was asked and I readily consented. How they appreciated me. Fondled and fingered me. I loved to be interfered with. It made me happy.

Fate of birth
25 December 1986

Mad people don't become all normal for Christmas Day. They don't hop out of bed and prepare a grand feast from a Delia Smith recipe, then play a game of charades and watch an afternoon film, munching on Brazil nuts. Christmas was like any other day at mine: wretched. None of that family life or warm home, just an empty shell with chilly rooms, faded furniture and a lot of mess. My mum was in bed, agitated and groaning as usual. No signs of the festive season: no presents, tinsel, mistletoe, a nut cracker, a bumper pack of Cadbury's Roses from the Co-op. The only sign I had that Christmas was here was the murmuring of the neighbour's television next door. Canned laughter from all those Christmas specials. I left the flat, hoping to catch someone else's Christmas. To be invited in somewhere, to belong.

I passed majestic houses adorned with decorations. A wreath, holly, a bunch of mistletoe. I took a nosy look into sumptuous front rooms at street level. Flowery patterned curtains, a grand piano. Sofas covered with plush cushions, the glow of a roaring fire. A Christmas tree in the corner, its white lights glowing. The ground floor rooms, empty of people; the basement, full of life. Gleaming fitted kitchens, a woman cooking, children squabbling, a plate of nibbles ready for eating.

I'd like some of that.

A teenage girl ran past me and disappeared through the front door. *Who are you, teenage girl? You look just like me, with your long blonde hair and skinny legs. But you seem so content, so carefree. What have I done to not be you? To not have your life? Where did I go wrong?*

I shuffled to the next house and stared up at another stunning tree. 'Happy, happy Christmas, sad girl!' it said, twinkling at me. Another, no tinsel this time, just exquisite glass birds and delicate little bells. I passed one house after another, every tree slightly different. Every year the same, every year this woe. I wanted to collapse, my ache was too great, too heavy to carry on.

Teenage girl, please let me in, let me be part of your family. Your father can feel my fanny if he wants to, just let me in. I will oblige for that roast, open wide for that sing-song, suck cock for that cracker, you just have to let me in!

I drank myself stupid and passed out in the street. The next morning the teenage girl and her well-to-do mother saw me lying there in a crumpled mess.

'That girl is a drain on the system,' she muttered to her daughter, as she stepped over me.

Dear Well-to-do Mother,

Please don't call me a drain on the system, there was a fault in the system that made me this way; a fault that I fell foul of because of a lack of understanding, observation and training among those who should have been looking after me. I'm not lying in my own sick because I am lazy, I'm lying in my own sick because I was paralytic last night. I was fucked by a fault in the system, the drink helps me forget.

I wish I could be like your daughter, she seems so happy. I so want to pick myself up, cut out half my brain and get rid of this pain. Put my rank clothes into a service wash and get a life. But I can't, it's not that black and white. You seem such a smart lady, so don't be so bloody ignorant. How old do you think I am? Look at my smooth skin under the smeared make-up. My young body under the barely black tights and the Lycra. There's the face of a child under this ruined bleached hair of home highlights kits. Me lying here in the gutter could have happened to anyone. It could have happened to your very own daughter. So please don't be harsh towards me, put your nose in the air and step over me. Help me to pick

myself up. I want to get off this path given to me in
life. Fate of birth. I did not choose it, it chose me.

Price upon application

I was naive in thinking shagging others would mean I'd get rid of Matthew.

'Give me some money!' I ordered. He was delighted to oblige for his favourite hole.

'I knew you'd call me again, you need me,' he said. He was right, he understood me. I did need him, even though I fought it. 'Do your crab,' he whispered. I remembered how wild he went when I was open.

I raised my body into an arch, with difficulty; I was not as supple as I used to be. I responded to his licks by jerking my fanny to his face with pretend enthusiasm, while he manically wanked. I hated those noises he made, grunts and slurps. Still I jerked harder, I might as well get something from it. *I'll come soon, unless his tongue gets tired, then he'll use his nose. Yep, there goes the nose. He'll want to finish me off.*

He lifted me up and entered me. *I wonder if he still goes limp with the guilt of raping a minor? Yuck, no, he doesn't.* Why would he? I am now of age.

With 20 quid I decided between medium-sliced white or a head fuck. I felt so worthless, I just wanted to get hammered. I walked into a corner shop and took the latter. Stupid, I could have had both.

I needed to ease off the drink, so I'd need less money, then I could finally stop seeing Matthew and the rest. But then I needed a little something to drink a little less. I wanted to try coke, speed is what I ended up with. It made me high after feeling low about fucking others for money. I was caught in a cycle, so I pulled myself together and found a proper job, cleaning toilets in a local B&B.

Greed
New Year's Day 1987

It was dark down there, the basement light like twilight. The sound of my metal bucket scraping on the cracked ceramic tiles was a welcome in the silence. I was trying to make money like normal people do. It was double time on New Year's Day and I was going straight.

'No more men,' I hummed to myself, as I held my nose with one hand, scrubbed out the shitty men's toilets with a big yellow glove on the other. *Bloody hell, the Gents smell rank.*

The manager came to see how I was getting on. He knew how I was getting on, he'd only been down here half an hour ago. He was nervous, he had that look in his eyes. I know that look. I always have that look in mine.

Manager, please, I'm trying to get away from all that, can't you see? I'm an addict of many madnesses, desperate to kick bad habits. I don't need people like you around me, tempting me when I am weak. Instead of offering to pay me for certain services, why don't you just help me?

He held out cash and the greed took over. *Bugger cleaning bloody toilets*, I thought, as I snapped the glove off.

'I want the television on,' I demanded, as I sauntered up the stairs holding my money tight. I hated myself, I had given in to my weakness, but at least I was still in control.

He jangled his keys and hurriedly took me to an empty bedroom. *Clean sheets, mmm, how I loved that smell of clean sheets.* He drew the curtains while I pulled off my clothes and put a cushion under my hips to raise me. I was so small compared to him. Then his hands were *all* over me. I got off on his excitement.

So turned on he was, I could tell he'd not had such a young one before. He went ape over my tits and could hardly contain himself when he was faced with my neat fanny. I guess he'd wanted me from the moment he saw my blonde hair, wondering to himself if my collars and cuffs matched. They didn't, not that he could see much, there was only about a millimetre of hair growth from my latest shave. But he could feel it prickling his fingers as he slid enthusiastically into my juices. He told me to pretend I was younger.

'I don't have to,' I said.

He absolutely loved that. Dirty man – they're all the same.

I turned round, arched and waited. He squealed like a girl and thrusted. I pushed against him, helping him further in, making stupid high-pitched noises that I knew he'd like, same old story. Bored, I seized the remote, turned up the volume and zoned out while my body carried on. I so made his New Year and I even got to see a bit of a fine old classic – *It's a Wonderful Life*.

This is all I am really good for, I thought, crunching on a walnut as he plunged into me for what seemed like the hundredth time. My soul had died long ago. What was wrong with me? Instead of running away from these situations I gravitated towards them. With every fuck, it confirmed what I thought of myself: a skank. I felt comfortable with what I knew, I wasn't scared. He could hurt me if he wanted. I didn't care.

He probed my other orifice.

'Oh, no, I've never done *that* before!' I lied. 'You'd be the very first.'

'Jesus! Please?'

'Umm, not sure. It'll be ever so tight. Look at you, you're so big, you might not fit.'

I was good at this dirty talk. He was as big as a horse about to bolt. He'd be one plunge, maybe two, then he'd be done.

I greased up and moved into place. I winced then tried to relax. *Manager, don't you feel guilty?*

I felt so full, so violated, so low. What I really wanted was a sugar daddy not a fare. I wanted to go out with men who'd look after me, not degrade me. But I also wanted a TV.

I allowed him all the way in.

'Oh my God!' he gasped and came. God had nothing to do it with it, Matthew did, he had taught me. Very useful knowledge in such a situation.

Doing a Diana
February 1987

'I really am seeing someone else,' I said to Matthew proudly. I had said it many times before, but he'd never taken me seriously. Now he seemed to be permanently parked up outside my mum's flat, flashing his headlights, praying I'd see and join him for a joy ride.

Not any more.

As a rule I wasn't into upper-class people, they seemed to be rather up themselves. I was usually only into done-well-out-of-adversity people. But Crispin was different. He was a handsome hulk of a man, much larger and stronger than Matthew. We had met in Picasso's cafe in Chelsea. A Sloane who liked a bit of council and just loved my dirty banter.

'Don't think you're getting into my knickers, cause I'm not wearing any,' I cracked.

'Hilarious!' he replied and begged to escort me to the Admiral Codrington, a right royal pub packed with hoorays slurping Bloody Marys. I thought I'd better make more of an effort to look like his kind. So at a time when every other girl wanted to be Madonna, I decided to do a Diana. I donned a string of fake pearls and wore a stripy shirt. I already had the shoes and the skirt, somehow an Alice band didn't suit me.

Matthew cried like a baby down the phone when I refused to see him that night.

'I don't want to, besides, I'm on a date,' I sneered.

'I can't bear not seeing you. I can't sleep. I love you!'

I needed to hear that at the home, not now, you fool.

He remained in his car with half a bottle of whisky to console him. I never smelt it on his breath, perhaps it was bought for show.

Unbeknown to Matthew, Crispin had parked his flashy white Golf right behind his big yellow Ford. Crispin honked the horn and I came running out into his muscly arms. I was 16 and he was 30. A fresh new 'daddy' to play with.

Snogging feverishly for all to see, I ignored the middle-aged paedophile with his head bowed in the driver's seat of his shitsville car. His dick now droopy. *He won't be feeding me with that any more.*

At that moment I felt as if I'd freed myself from one oldie to another. I could never control Matthew, however hard I tried, but I vowed I'd control this man. Through my years of grooming, I had learnt how to use my body to manipulate men. Now I decided I would use it to my advantage, turn myself around through dirty sex, and end up rich. I was so over being poor. I had big plans for myself, I would not die as I had been born, a victim in waiting.

As I hopped into my new ride's convertible and

sang along to Duran Duran, I saw Matthew driving off, probably to find some other youngster to fiddle with. *I must find the courage to tell the police, to save others. It's too late to save myself.*

Matthew turned up the next day with prezzies. Bracelets, earrings, a necklace with my initials on it. MM. I snatched the gifts off him and slammed the door in his face, making sure he could hear me mocking. *Fucking wanker.* Now I wasn't afraid of him any more, I took advantage.

Hungry, I called him to take me for my favourite margherita. With my needs satisfied and his not, I slipped out the fire exit and giggled when he drove furiously alongside trying to catch me up. As I approached home, I knew he was there by the sound of the Steve Miller Band playing on his radio when the traffic was still. *Piss off!* I thought. But I was bored. I went up to the flat and waited for his knock. *Knock knock.* A pause. *Knock knock.*

I opened the door and let him in. I then waltzed around my room in my practically see-through white broderie anglaise knickers. He loved them: he would, he'd bought them. He had spent hours in the shop fingering the lingerie till he was leaking and I was laughing and the assistant was alarmed.

With my bedroom door firmly closed, I pushed my bottom against his boner, my knickers slipping up my arse, where he so wanted to be. I knew he wouldn't dare, my mother was head-banging the wall in the next room. He might have grabbed my cunt like a cock and squeezed it, but he knew he couldn't take the risk of actually fucking me.

Instead I teased, 'Here, come feed my mouth.'

I exposed his knob and licked the tip gently, ever so gently, just how he liked it, till it spat pre-come, while his shark eyes darted nervously back and forth to my bedroom door. Then I pulled my knickers right up my cunt till the fabric disappeared inside my lips. I shoved it higher and higher, making the cloth wet as I rubbed it against my clit. His mouth was dribbling. He so wanted to eat me. Hearing my mother babbling in the hall I then told him to fuck off out of it.

'Go finish yourself off with your wife, I have someone else in my life!'

And then the letters came. Huge scribbling scrawly writing full of clichéd emotions telling me how much he missed me. Matthew used a fountain pen, was that supposed to impress me? I used one of his missives to clear the shit from the toilet that had blobbed down the bowl and plopped on the floor. Not my shit, my mother's. His poem didn't flush, his words clogged the system. I had to pull that trite trash out with another which I used as a glove; protection for my delicate little hands.

You are so special. I was so lucky to have met you.

These lies did not grab my interest. I couldn't respond to his attempts to fuck with my brain, he had already fucked the whole of me. Never mind his nose, his big toe had been half the way up my arse.

I needed more, more than he could give me now.
Matthew, you are getting boring.

Point of entry

That night Crispin got the ride of his life and I got lots of cash.

'I'd like to see you naked in your pearls,' he said, grinning like a naughty boy.

'Well, I like to rub them along my slit, one by one.' That was a lie, they were new, but I thought I'd say it anyway. I pulled them back and forth, back and forth, then put them in my mouth. He liked that. I used them as a horse's bit, he held the rest as reins as he nervously entered my arse from behind.

'Are you sure?' he asked politely. I then asked him for money while he was still in shock at how tight it was and how willing I'd been.

That was to hook you, you gullible Sloane!

When it gets to point of entry I can sort of enjoy it now but my arse used to be much tighter. I do sphincter exercises at traffic lights hoping it will help.

In his Sloaney voice he confided, 'Uhh, I've never actually, like, done *that* before you know, babe.'

'You've been missing out, honey,' I smiled. I think I was a bit too kinky for him though. He didn't like it when I called him 'Daddy'.

'How about just the once then?' I pleaded with my Cheshire Cat grin.

'Uhmm, not overly keen,' he replied. It didn't do anything for him, he said. It wouldn't, would it, but it did something for me.

I twirled my hair and stroked his chest. With his arms wrapped around me, I pressed myself to him, caressed his balls, and said in a language he'd understand, 'I wish I could afford to buy my Mum a birthday present, she's, like, having such a hard time.'

He shot up with a semi, grabbed his cords and pulled out a wad from his wallet.

'Gosh, poor you, of course,' he said.

Bingo! A rich Sloane, not a tight one. My cunt throbbed when he thrust those notes my way. I had the urge to finish myself off against his groin, but gratitude came first. I made him big and, with me already dribbling, sat on him. 'Let me thank you, darling,' I whispered, but he knew from the way I bucked, that that fuck was really for me. His hands pushed down on my hips, helping me rock faster and said the words I wanted to hear, 'Come for Daddy, you know you want to.'

He's *such a pushover,* I thought, confused by my multiple orgasm. Why does the word 'Daddy' turn me on? Because I don't have one? Pushing those awkward thoughts aside, I took another fiver when he was taking a piss. *Will I always be a skank?*

Back at the flat, Matthew was waiting outside. I let him in. That was stupid, my mother was out. He got his own back for my last tease, stuffing my soiled knickers into my mouth, *yuck, couldn't they be in his?* I recoiled.

He fucked me hard, so hard. He was so big, like a leech full of blood about to explode. Couldn't it be the teeniest bit of fun for me? *Bang, bang, bang.* I was tearing now. I guess I deserved it. Did I need stitches?

'Disappointing,' he said. 'You're not as tight as you used to be.'

He then became all gentle. He read out a letter he had written for me. I could see him searching my face for a hint of hope that I would soften, let him in my heart again. He used to have it, I don't quite know how or why that feeling for him stopped. His neediness was so unattractive. But his dominance I adored. I might think I wanted the power, but it didn't fulfil me. I liked being brutalised.

'I am leaving my wife,' he told me. There was a time when I would have been so happy to hear those words. Now I just thought, *Yeah, and..?* Because I had a new boyfriend.

I really liked Crispin. He was polite and charming and somehow respectful of me. Perhaps it was his public school upbringing. I found my heart melting even as I fleeced him. He had a cracking smile and a strong jaw and floppy hair like a surfer dude from Cornwall. He was sweet, he had this vulnerability about him. His eyes widened at every new sex trick, he was discovering another world. So was I, a world of Rolexes, gopping cufflinks and family signet rings. Of course that embossed falcon or whatever it was went straight up my cunt. In between my fingers going straight up his arse. I gave the ring back eventually. I washed it with spit first and slipped it back on. He guffawed and fucked hard where it had been.

As time went on, Crispin could see a pattern emerging. I knew exactly what I was doing, now he did too. Porn sex followed by requests for money for some poor relative's birthday, always the same.

'You have a lot of relatives,' he joked. He must have thought giving me the odd bit of spending money was worth it though, he did get my bare pussy in his face.

What was this obsession with a hairless pussy? In X-rated films and magazines, there it was. Over and over again. I was constantly shaving to keep up. I needed to be less of a wimp and wax. Crispin loved how smooth I was, loved me looking like a little girl, probably turned him on more, even though he'd never admit it. Maybe that's why he called me 'baby' in the sack.

Over time my respect for him was waning. *Paedophile, paedophile, paedophile,* I unfairly thought, seeing as I was now over the age of consent. *Abuser, abuser,* I teased in my head, with every stroke of his dick in my arse. Just as well I was so used to being violated there, seeing as it was now his favourite position. If he loved anuses so much, why didn't he just fuck a man?

'Gay, gay, gay,' I breathed, when my finger slid deep into his arse. I then dribbled on the entrance and swapped it for my thumb. I tried to wank him with the other hand, but I couldn't get the rhythm right. Crispin took over and came loudly with my thumb pumping with such velocity I nearly sprained it.

'That was awesome, babe.' It was now the only way he came. I had spoilt him.

I nicked his Rolex Oyster Perpetual, couldn't help myself, there it was as he lay passed out, his dick pissing in the wind. I had to have it. He was perplexed the next morning, 'Where did I leave it?' he cried. 'Here, help me find it. Daddy gave it to me.'

Oh dear! I felt bad because he had already given me a Tag Heuer, but not that bad when I realised a Tag wasn't as expensive as a Rolex. I thought I'd better let him find his watch behind his bedstead. His good core values had rubbed off on me.

Losing interest in Crispin, I began to enjoy seeing Matthew waiting outside. Saying goodbye to Crispin knowing Matthew would then knock on the door. *Knock knock*. A pause. *Knock knock*. I liked that fear of Matthew coming to get me, his weight on top of me. His threats, the thrill of finding him disgusting, of not being able to breathe. 'Get off me!' I cried. When I knew really he loved me.

When my mum was out I would ring him to come over. He was thrilled. He'd be all coy with limp flowers from the petrol station. I would then make him jealous with my endless chattering about Crispin giving me carnations, so he would be rough once more. Matthew was confused; I was in heaven.

Fresh ink from his letters would be under his thumbnails and on his skin. I'd think of that ink being cleaned by my saliva while I looked into his shark eyes and sucked his thumb again. I spat it out; sure enough, the ink was nearly all gone. That same thumb circled my clit when I was on his knee. I thought of God's helper when Matthew was making circles, a thought of horror that Matthew erased through pleasure till I came.

'Now suckle me,' he said.

I stuck out my tongue. Was it black?

'Blow on me, Matthew, blow on me,' I asked absentmindedly. I got down from his lap and positioned myself over his face and eased down. I bucked while he blew. I was letting go.

I thought the ink from my tongue would poison me, punishing me for those disgusting thoughts that turned to Matthew whenever I wanted quick relief. Whenever I imagined him I dripped. I fought it as I knew it was wrong. But then I felt myself throbbing. I couldn't help touching, arching, gaping, rubbing, gasping his name. That licking. Then I sucked my thumb and convulsed.

Matthew, Go away. GO AWAY! Will you ever go away?

Then I hurt myself.

Sleazy Sloanes
May 1987

I was never faithful to Crispin. I could make more money if I saw other posh boys too. It was profitable appearing to be a Sloane. I was only ever interested if they were loaded. Some were so tight they wouldn't even buy me a cappuccino, that sort of attitude didn't get far with me. Instead, I'd hike down to a club in Chelsea and single out the ones ordering champagne. I'd sit at the bar and wait till they inevitably spotted me. It was always the slightly sleazy Sloaney ones that did. Only a matter of time before they took the girl with fake pearls back to their flats in Fulham for what they'd hoped for: a damn good fuck or, at the very least, release. But all they got was a yummy suck of my nipples and a little tease, till I knew I'd be more than a one-night stand. I'd make more money that way, even more if I was up for a threesome.

One had a good thing going: two willing girls wanting him. 'Eeny meeny miney mo, which one first, I'll give you both a go!' His other fuck-buddy had much bigger tits than me, she was bigger all over, I noticed, but he wasn't looking at her fat arse while shafting her; he was staring at her tits jiggling, jiggling from her writhing, writhing from me teasing her clit. He then took me from behind, so I could carry on licking her and he could carry on watching her tits till he came, she came and I came from her returning the favour.

'I like something I can hold on to,' he told me. 'You're too skinny.'

I definitely had a bit of problem, skinny minny me, who would not even think about eating till this particular man said he wanted a real woman to fuck, not a child. Flesh and tits were desired, I'd say he saved me from anorexia.

I didn't join them that many more times though, I didn't like him preferring her to me. It was becoming rather tedious witnessing the look of ecstasy on his face as he wanked over her pornographic tits.

I decided never again to have a threesome with a girl whose tits were bigger than my own. At the same time I started saving for a tit job. It might take years but something bigger would open more doors than my pert pillows. Get rid of a few paedophiles anyway.

I laughed at them all with my discreet indiscretions. Such a thrill, waking up in the morning to find some trust funder slipping in and out of my fanny, freaking him out by shouting 'Dada', while fucking in a frenzy for the craic. He'd give me a bit of spending money, I'd then bugger off without a shower and go and provoke some other unworldly man. So irresponsible. His come mixing with another's, he gave me cash too. 'I want to look after you,' he'd say. *Yeah right, more like you want me to finger you.*

These men were putty in my hands once I did that. Apparently no posh girl went near their smelly arses, that trick wasn't on the straight girl's agenda. I leant over and searched for their anuses with my index finger. I scratched their rim with my nail. With not much coaxing, I pushed in violently. Soon my finger became a vibrator, as they didn't like the chocolate bar I suggested.

'Too messy, darling.'

Shame, could have got rid of that fetid smell. I tried a thick black candle, plunging deeper.

'Steady on!' they cried.

I imagined the candle was a knife, 'I want to hurt you,' I taunted.

Stab, stab, stab.

'Ow!' I soothed their pain with a gentle lick, then giggled and decided to grow my nails.

After sex, I'd request cash, with my puppy eyes wanting. My lips surrounding their hard-ons to say 'Thank you' twice in one day.

I must always say 'Thank you', Matthew had taught me that.

'Manners! Where are your manners!' he cried when he gave me the latest slimline camera from Brent Cross. Now I opened up automatically when I was given money, even after I had done the deed. Was that prostitution? Yes, but a more subtle version. It didn't make me feel half as bad about myself. I hardly ever fucked *complete* strangers for money any more, urging them to, 'Rape me!'

That fantasy made me wet, it made me ashamed, it made me want to come.

Strength of a thousand men
March 1988

Our cooker was on fire, the smell of smoke choked me. My mum stared at the flames, grinning. 'I want an adventure!' she whispered.

'Let's just start with putting out the flames, shall we?' I replied, wetting a towel to throw over the hob.

I have to get away from this ill human being. Forever naked and crying to herself. Not grasping that I am in front of her as she desperately tries to find the door to get out, to escape the nastiness in her head. *But Mum, the nastiness follows you.*

I noticed bruises on her breasts, marks on her wrists. She punched and she cut, punishing herself for who knew what crime. I worried that she might go further, her mind was more fragile than mine. I pushed past her and ran out of the flat, double-locking the door behind me before she could follow.

She banged her fists angrily on the glass. I rushed down three flights of stairs to get fucked, forget what I had left behind. I couldn't let her out of the flat again, it would have been the third time she'd been found naked in Ladbroke Grove. But that behaviour alone was not enough to section her.

'She has to be a danger to herself or others under section 3 of the Mental Health Act,' I was told. Surely aiming a knife at herself, then at me, pronouncing, 'I will end our suffering of simply being women,' was enough?

'Women,' she muttered. Then she started to wave the knife to spell out the word. 'W. O. M. E. N. The word "men" is in "women". Men will always be in women, see? I can't escape, I can't escape. Men will always be in MEEEEE!' she went on, now thrashing about.

I called the mental health team and they turned up with doctors and the police in a van, not an ambulance. How insensitive.

'She needs a hospital bed, not a police cell,' I shouted, upset. *What will the neighbours say?* Too late for that thought. Anyway, I couldn't care about them, I had to think about my own self-preservation.

I was so over this situation. I didn't feel unhappiness any more, just irritation at this sicko. *Mum, you are draining the life out of me.* I did not need this appendage, this child to look after. A child looking after a child, how ridiculous. So many times I wanted to put a pillow over her head as she kept me awake, ranting till dawn.

I couldn't stand the anguish in her voice. I wanted to end her suffering, help her when she tried to drown herself in the bath. Seeing her face under the water with her eyes closed, her mouth tightly shut, holding her breath for as long as she could, I should have put my hands on both her shoulders and held her down until she went floppy. She could have had peace then. Her bruised body could rest from self-harm. Her face could be serene for the first time in years. I didn't want to be thumped any more by this wailing nutter. 'You have been poisoned!' she told me. 'Poisoned from passing through my dirty filthy hole!'

The mental health team were reluctant to section her, maybe because it cost so much money. But it was obvious my mum was in distress. She had the strength of a thousand men as they tried to grab her. She reacted violently. We were all in danger, it seemed.

'You traitor!' she shouted at me. 'You fucking whore, I will never forgive you!' I was impressed, this outburst was a rare moment of lucidity. She lashed out at me and had to be restrained, like a wild animal. The police finally bowed her head into the van. *So indecent.*

I laughed nervously at her fat face being carted off. I couldn't possibly have cried, I'd never have stopped.

She was gone – the relief! A month of peace and quiet and some legal money. I cashed her giros every week and pretended the flat was my own.

I was mature. I spent her money on food and noticed the gas was about to be cut off. I didn't have time to save up and I hated not having a bath. Posh boy with the bottomless wallet was away, I'd dumped Crispin and there was no way I was calling Matthew. So I went up the borough to a place where I always found someone.

'I want to gorge on your penis,' I told my latest stranger. *Really, I want to cut you.*

I thought of all that bubbling hot water and how I was going to scrub my body clean. He went down on me and I responded well to his lickings for that money. I didn't tell the bloke I had my period though, he was too turned on by my bare flesh to notice. Couldn't he taste the difference? Perhaps he thought all young clits tasted of blood. I smelt like a butcher's shop that day.

'You're so lovely, so… so fresh,' he kept telling me. *Your first young cunt, more like.*

'Come destroy me, baby,' I begged. He nipped me with his sharp teeth on my shoulder.

He left without looking in the mirror, my blood all over his face. Shame it wasn't from me slicing him, that nip bloody hurt. Next time. But he never returned, served him right, asking me to pretend I was prepubescent. *Hope he dies!*

I think I will ring Matthew next time. I hope there isn't a next time, but I know I am trapped by his security if all else fails.

There will always be a next time.

Pass the parcel

Taking in the hollow face of my next fuck. The smell of smoke, bottles of beer and lube lined up. A hard-faced woman summoned me to sit on her lap and cradle her empty tits while she fingered me.

'Here, let me nurse you,' she cooed, shoving her inverted nipple in my mouth. 'Suck me,' she cried. I dried up. She pushed me on the bed and positioned her flabby bush right on top of mine. Rubbing fast and hard, she tried to arouse my clit. Her tits were on my face, suffocating me. She raised her arse and some creep's fingers entered her anus, pushing her body further into mine. The creep crawled over to my head and positioned himself. His foul smell made me feel sick as his balls brushed my hair while he wanked.

'Lick me!' he demanded. I couldn't reach as I was crushed by the weight of his other hand, placed on my head to steady himself. He shoved his fingers in my mouth, pushing me hard into the pillow. They tasted of shit, hers.

He watched her tits swing back and forth, with every bash of her fanny on to mine. He sucked his teeth and dribbled. Come trickled down her tits, dripped off one nipple on to my hair. *Sticky, so icky.*

This was too much, they were on something. I wanted it too. I begged and at last they gave it to me. My first line of coke, straight up my nose. The second, up my fanny. The third, not coke, something else, up my arse. I lost all my inhibitions, relaxed, relented and performed like a puppet. It was good. I was a slippery eel with come all over me.

I heard voices, movement. More had entered the room. I was auctioned off for fun. Passed like a parcel, a layer of skin ripped with every turn. I couldn't get enough, until they blindfolded me. Blurred faces whispering to me.

'Who is it?' I said. 'I can't see you!'

What does it matter? I am wanted.

I felt duty bound to see my mum in the mental health unit. I could never get used to the difference in her when she was sent to these places. From super hyper to ultra calm, floating down the hospital hall. Drugs are amazing. Shame the doctors couldn't force her to take them when her stint in hospital was up. What was the point of sectioning her when she went back to her frenetic behaviour within a fortnight of coming out? I saw her throw her pills in the bin. Stupid waste of money, effort and time, she needed longer.

I was told that being mentally ill is a bit like being an alcoholic. My mum needed to gain an insight into her illness in order to combat it. She had to admit that she had a problem first, but she was nowhere near that.

I wished I could tell people that she was doolally. They'd make fun though, calling me 'nutty' too. I wanted to change their views. But if I said, 'It's a chemical imbalance of the brain,' they looked at me blankly. So I tried to explain. 'My mum is like a person with, say, a type of flu, who needs antibiotics to get better. But she doesn't have flu, she has an illness of the mind, and needs mood stabilisers to get better. They don't get her completely better though, but they do enable her to have a relatively normal life.' In earnest I would add: 'It's ignorance that makes you afraid. Don't be scared of mad people, they can't help it. My mum, if she was rational, would say she doesn't want to be this way. She wants to be well, like you. Think of her as sort of disabled in the head.'

This went way over my friends' heads. Far too heavy, but it was worth a try. It seemed that anything to do with a disease of the mind was taboo. I wished Mum had cancer, there would be no shame in that. At least then I could talk about it. *And when she died, I'd be nobody's carer, I would be free.*

I made the flat nice for her return. I tidied up the jumble and decorated her room with flowers picked from the graveyard. I'd missed her.

*

I felt quite sorry for Matthew now, he was hankering for me, ringing me, demanding to see me. When I eventually allowed him in, he cried in my lap and sucked my thumb, *my* thumb now. He hated that I had withdrawn from him. He then pulled my thighs apart. I let him. He pushed away my knickers and started licking, his snot mixing with my mucous. Then I heard his usual murmurings.

'Does it take your mind off your sorrow?' I patronised as I stroked his receding hair. I tried to hump his face to satisfy him, but found it difficult to come, he seemed so much smaller, weaker. How could I possibly orgasm with a man who sucked my thumb?

Matthew, stand up like a man, rape like a man should rape. Where's the pain? Pinch me, bite me, hurt me. I want to be humiliated. That's better. I want it harder. Faster, faster!

And I thought of my mother while I bled.

Mum,

I don't really want you to die, I want you to get better. I want to see you smile again. A real smile, the kind that makes the sides of your eyes crinkle, then I'll know you have come back to me. But you never will, will you? The mum who smiled while singing 'Tambourine Man' is dead.

My confidence had disappeared, Matthew sensed it. *Knock knock.* A pause. *Knock knock.*

'Here my little baby, I've brought you a dummy.'

'That's not even funny,' I said in a miserable mood.

'Come here and say thank you,' he suggested, moving forward.

'Fuck off!' I heard myself shout.

He overpowered me and stuffed the dummy in my mouth. I looked into his shark eyes and automatically started sucking. I was a child again, I let him take over. He lay me on the bed, gently pulled up my man-sized T-shirt, put his face to my fanny and peered. I didn't know why I fought him. I always gave in, always kept my cunt bare for his call. I felt safe now. I took the dummy from my mouth and inserted the teat into my hole. He took it from me, tasted it, and entered me. I wet myself. He had brought me to orgasm, like no one else could. Leaving me in shame.

I cried.

Mum, I want to be a child again.

Bingo
May 1989

The council gave me the keys to a flat of my very own. Of course I didn't accept any old thing, I'd learnt that from my mother. 'No concrete or estates, period dwellings only,' I demanded. I'm surprised the housing officer didn't tell me to piss off.

It's very hard to get a flat from the council, I was ever so lucky, I knew that. But I had so many points from being in a children's home, my mum being a danger and from us nearly being evicted again. She hadn't filled out the housing benefit forms; it was fortunate I found them, filled them out and forged her signature.

It was a tiny flat, in a stucco-fronted building, six stories high with no lift and no heating. The communal hallway was unloved and the neighbours had their own problems, no doubt, but it was a gorgeous little space to me. My own place, peace from a howling nutter, my darling mother. I sat on the bare floorboards and cried, it felt like I'd won the bingo. My first step to a normal, happy life.

Living on my own was an easy transition, there was no one but me to think about. Sorting the bills, changing a bulb or a fuse on a plug with Radio 1 for company. Cooking the basics did not phase me, I had done it lots. This time it was a doddle because I'd got an essential moving-in pack when I got my flat. Kitchen utensils, pots, pans and 100 coloured tea towels paid for by the council rehab scheme for kids out of care. Maybe I would get a fitted kitchen one day.

Before I'd left, my mother had made me feel very drained. I'd almost given up on her ever being well again. A cloud crept over me whenever I thought about her, so apart from making sure she was getting her benefits, I couldn't give her much more. I felt as if her siblings should have taken over, but it seemed they couldn't deal with her. Or me.

'Why don't you call in on us?' my relatives had the audacity to say, when I ran into them in the Portobello Road. 'Come see your cousins.'

I used to be so proud to be part of this family. Proud of my history, even if all it gave me was grief. On St Patrick's Day, you dragged me round the Gaelic pubs wearing nothing but the colour green, placing coins in collections for The Cause. Bleating 'Up da RA' to anyone you met, whether they were listening or not. Then all you did was drink Guinness and sang songs that we wanted to slit our wrists by on a badly tuned guitar.

'I'm a miserable Paddy from the Emerald Isle, and I'm gonna hang myself in a while, because I cannot, for the life of me, make this ballad rhyme.'

I was not amused and by midnight I'd be curled up with my coat as a teddy bear.

I now have cousins I hardly know because I find it too upsetting to see them. Casualties of war.

100 stone

There was not even one single 'Welcome to your new home' card from any of my rellies. *Bastards.* But I kept busy, filling my flat with carefully chosen cushions, carefully chosen rich men.

I had nearly replaced all that Matthew had given me. But he was still not out of my life for good, appearing one day with that same double knock on the door.

'I brought you a house-warming gift,' he said, with that same expectant grin.

'Piss off!' I replied, trying to break his spell.

I'll see you when I want to see you. I'll not be a child again.

I took the gift anyway and he offered to put a new lock on my front door. 'But only if you're paying,' I said, with my sweetest sideways smile.

My men took me to upmarket shops and bought me accessories for my flat. I soon developed a taste for more expensive items of furniture. I longed for a leather chair from Conran, a corner sofa from Habitat. Acquaintances wondered how I could afford these designer goodies. They presumed I had a rich daddy. I never confirmed nor denied that theory.

I was beginning to have middle-class aspirations, but it takes more than money and taste to go up a class. I needed to be educated. Fucking Sloanes had inspired me, they had degrees. Now I wanted one too, to go to art school, to be like one of them. The teachers at my old school had always said, 'You are bright, just hindered by your home life.' *Yes I am clever*, I thought, *I can do this.*

Determination kicked in. I studied hard for an A level in art and prepared for an interview. 'You'll never get in to art school,' said one of my boys. I bit his cock and studied harder. Eventually I was offered an interview. I got it. Must have been the short skirt and biker boots that did it. Or was it the way I looked at the interviewer? *Had we… ever?*

Just as well it wasn't a woman assessing me. Women don't like me because I don't put on the charm for them. What's the point? It'd be wasted. I treated myself to an ice cream. Could it be that I genuinely had talent? I was on the road to joining the educated classes. I celebrated by writing a card to myself pretending it was from my mother.

Well done you!
Lots of kisses,
Mum x x x

Didn't sound like her. What did she 'sound' like anyway? I scribbled it out and wrote instead,

Congratulations my darling, I am so proud of you!
With all my love,
Mum x

So banal. I think she'd be more original. In big letters I scratched,

Whore, whore, you fucking whore!

So hard into the paper, the ballpoint nearly broke. Who was I kidding anyway? She wouldn't have written at all. I threw the paper on the floor and went to see her.

Mum, Mum are you in?
     I didn't like coming back here, to this gloomy hallway outside her flat. It brought me terrible pain, a lead weight in my stomach, I felt 100 stone. Staring at a chipped blue

door that never seemed to open. Behind it, a mother that never sent a card.

Crack
September 1990

On arrival at art school, I was aware I was a few years older than the other students, more knowing, like a mature student. Most were kids fresh from gap years with posh voices and polo shirts, ponies and Daddy's credit card. I envied their wide-eyed wonder and excitement about their first term. They were in residential student halls, I was in my council flat. Art school was so much fun for them, it felt a bit like going to work to me. When I came home, my student life ended. For them, it carried on. They were all living together, listening to INXS, one big party.

I was resentful. I went home and listened to the Cure. If I'd wanted a real student life of staying in halls, who would have paid for me to keep my home when I returned at the end of term? I couldn't have afforded both while they could just go back to 'Mummy'. It hit me, too, how much I'd missed out on. Music concerts, clothes shopping with friends, ice skating, the cinema, hanging out in Kensington Market. Playing, just being. Having that first fumble with a boy my own age, that first kiss. My first orgasm was with Matthew. *I wish it had been with anyone else but him.*

I went from a child to an adult in one day, Matthew made sure of that. The other students went from Mummy to art school, pocket money to allowance. It's not fair, I felt like I was an old person in a young person's body. I looked like them but never would be them and that's how it was going to be for the rest of my life. I'd always be living on a parallel line, looking in, never crossing over – detached. I had nothing in common with anyone, so I didn't even try. I walked alone and just did what I knew how to do: provoke.

I stole from those students with their happy lives. It made me feel so much better. A stupid little notebook, a glove. A useless thing to me, very frustrating for them. I wouldn't want to be sitting next to me. I progressed to money. The odd fiver for a cocktail. Not nice, that was almost a week's beans on toast for them.

The students went off to a rave, I to a bar. They had their first taste of weed, I had my first taste of cocaine burnt on a spoon. Thank God I didn't like it, thank fuck I felt I didn't need it. A friend who did died alone, found decaying in a flat, days later.

The boys wanted more than just alcohol, and I could get it. If only I had the guts to be a dealer, I wouldn't need to be a hole any more. But I didn't. What if I went to prison? Visiting hours, endless check-ups. Doors banging one behind the other. I had a fear of institutions, your life is not your own in one of those. Rules and regulations, lights out when you're not ready, rape when you're asleep? No thank you.

I wore tight clothes and short skirts to art school to silent disapproval from the girls. I didn't care what they thought of me, but the lecturer, I'm sure he fancied me, his eyes moved with me. The student boys seemed to be scared of me, looking awkward as I swished past. I blamed that dirty look in my eye, my lack of knickers, perhaps they could smell me. I should give them a peek of my crack, something to think about for the weekend. *Dirty, disgusting men!*

Military man

I wanted to fuck women's fathers, brothers, husbands. I wanted no roses, no emotion, no ties, no affair, no fall out, just raw sex. I didn't want any mess, I fancied a fuck, why couldn't it be that easy? I had needs, just like a man.

I walked into a seedy party and saw another woman's husband salivate over my tight top. I loved playing games with a wandering eye. I brushed past him, and pressed my pubic bone into his thigh, pushing my tits into his tank top. I let him have an eyeful when I bent down to pick up my dropped-on-purpose drink. I stopped halfway, looked up and stared into his face with my obvious desire. 'While I'm down here, shall I?' I asked. I was open-mouthed, waiting to be fed. I saw his trousers twitch. It was so much fun winding him up. *Tosser!*

I was ready to gorge, gagging to be molested. I plopped down on to the lap of a portly balding chap and soon had him squirming in his seat. 'I'm gonna suck your dick like a dummy, little man. But first you're going lick my clit like it's a lolly.'

'You have my attention,' he quipped, in military speak. Playfully he pretended he was not affected by the filthy words I whispered. Gradually I coaxed him to one of the many bathrooms in the house with the promise of giving him his first ever line of speed. I told him it was coke. He'd led a sheltered life. Climbing into the bath I pulled my skirt up, parted my legs and let him see my slit open up to the pinkness. Then the piss, dribbling down my legs, disappearing into the plug hole. Laughing, I sprinkled a bit of powder on my labia and beckoned him to, 'Lick my bare cunt clean!'

He was shocked, yet I could see he was turned on by this performance. He started to leave.

'But you so want to stay,' I said, grabbing him. I dug my long fingernails into his wrinkly skin. 'You dirty, dirty old man. I can see you want to lick it because it looks like a little girl's!' I clutched the last remaining hairs on his head and pushed him down. Disgusted, he wrestled with me. I felt his hard-on as he manhandled me out of the way. I was left frigging myself, feeling satisfied that later he would be ashamed, trying desperately not to think of my pinkness while pumping his nice but dull wife harder than usual.

Fucking paedophile. I want to stab you.

I think I may have a problem, though not as bad as my mother's. She walked past me in Portobello looking in a right state, worse than usual, cackling manically. Somehow that laughing of hers seems so much more scary than someone swearing aggressively. I crossed over the road and followed her. I wanted to make sure this wasn't the day she died from skipping in front of a van; something smart, befitting for a snob, a van from Peter Jones should do. She'd be raging from the heavens if it was a white one with a tinker behind the wheel. 'Death from Skipping.' That would be the official verdict. Or maybe it would be 'Death from Dangerous Walking.' I had an urge to slip my arm in hers and take her to the park. She would have liked that years ago. Now she would just tell me I smelt, which would not be a lie. She'd call me a slag, she'd be about right now. 'Get away, get away!' she would shout. 'You're poison.' Quite astute is my mother.

Dark side

October 1991

I decided I had to stop using my cunt to get me through art school. *I'll be normal*, I told myself. I tried waitressing. God was I shit, I got more tips from bending over than for my crap service. But it was useful, I met another middle-aged man.

He was married. I talked while he buggered me. His wife never let him do that. I wondered if he was gay.

He was so delighted by my expertise, so elated he had found a body he could offload his desires on, he offered to pay my way. I agreed even though he got off on the fact I'd been in care.

'My poor baby, in a children's home,' he said, while on his knees studying my fanny. He opened my legs and started rubbing my clit with his fingers. I stared at him doe-eyed and responded.

Smiling, he asked, 'Did anyone take, you know, advantage of you, in there?'

I nodded with a forlorn look in my eyes. 'Uh huh, one of the social workers.'

'Really? Ooh, there, there,' he groaned delightedly. 'Now tell me what that big nasty social worker did to you!'

Exactly what you're doing to me.

'He'd tiptoe into my room at night, put his hands under the covers and slowly creep up and up.'

'Up, up, to where? Your hole? Did he then fiddle with you, like, this?' Rubbing harder.

'Yes!' I said, writhing.

'Ohh, you must have been so small. Did he then stretch your little hole with his fat fingers, like, this?' His digits entered me urgently.

'Oh yes!' I cried, mock ecstatic, to his clumsy pumping.

'Did he then mount you with his big, big penis, like, this?' He was on me now, violently pushing in.

'Ow! Yes!' *Just like that.*

'He must have seemed so huge, you must have been so tight. I need more detail!' he shouted.

'It hurt,' I replied. I was not enjoying this. 'So I sucked his thumb to soothe me.'

'Suck mine!' he demanded.

I obliged and he erupted.

It did not make me feel good about myself, him getting off on the rape of a minor. I hoped he wasn't a paedophile too. It was my fault, I should never have told him all that. But the married man claimed to feel sorry for me. I played up to it, of course.

'Yes, oh yes, poor little me, all alone,' I rasped.

As he dipped his dick in my sweetness, he whispered, 'I will look after you, my darling. My darr-r-r-ling.' I tightened my muscles. Matthew had a lot to answer for.

Saving, always saving for my tits to be made into a porn star's. *Think of those new tits*, I said to myself as I acted out yet another tedious scene from *Debbie Does Dallas*. I was far away daydreaming of my tit operation when I woke up to wetness between my cheeks.

Funny, he thought he was doing me the world of good by helping me. *Yes, married man, I will be your 'girl', but not because I like you stabbing me with your stubby member. It's your money and your wife that turns me on. I love that you are cheating on your lady who has it all. She needs to have a taste of real life. I'll make sure she finds out about us when I'm ready to get shot of you.*

That's not very nice of me, I thought. I must hate men, I conclude.

'Will you do something for me?' my married man asked, as I sat astride him. He was too embarrassed to say what it was but said he'd give me stacks. I squeezed his dick tighter and opened my legs further so he could see my Raspberry Delight. He stopped breathing. I looked into his eyes and whispered, 'You can request anything you want from me.' *But I will slice you if it's anything to do with children.*

'Violate me,' he replied.

Is that all?

I turned him over and then I became the man. 'I'm going to poke you till you bleed,' I cried. With no lubrication, I picked up a glass bottle and shoved it right up him. With every ram he screamed and screamed until he came. I picked out his shit from under my nails with the shank of my earring. I pretended he was Matthew. I think I may have torn into him a little too hard. But it turned me on to hear him in agony.

Money! Money! I now had lots of money! I spread it on my bed and lay on it, then inserted a rolled-up £20 note into my hole.

Eat your heart out Matthew, you only managed shoving a fiver up me, but I was a child then. I am one tough lady now, with a filthy hole to match.

I had lots saved for my new tits now. I was almost there.

Goodbye child-like me, goodbye sicko warped paedophiles, here's to a new me.

I needed this plastic surgery. I wanted to be rid of the feel of Matthew's touch. I wanted the surgeon to cut off the tits that he'd pawed, the cunt that he came on. Then I could make sure he never went near me again.

But I can't cut off my cunt, can I? I have to live with it. *It* follows me everywhere. I can't even look at it, it disgusts me. I want to stab it, kill myself with a knife by fucking it. I can't even look at my knickers. When I take them off, I throw them in the bin. Dirty, soiled, filthy and full of poison, that's my cunt.

I wish I had no cunt. I wish I'd been a boy then I would be clean. But I'm not a boy and I'm certainly not clean. I am the 'Any place, any time, anything, anywhere' girl. I am not here any more. I'll suck for food, fuck for fun. Shove a bottle up my cunt, I don't care, my mind is now elsewhere. Hit me, kick me, punch me if you want. My body has flown to the dark side.

Crate training
February 1992

A mangy mongrel stared at me from a dog crate in the corner of a room. Saliva dripped on to his paw as he watched my every move. Swiping dog food from a can, I smeared it over my fanny. Opening the door of the crate, I enticed the mongrel to come out.

'Here, doggy, here,' I said, laughing. *Jesus, could the beast disease me?*

My latest loser pulled the animal away, spun me round and manhandled me into the dog crate, scraping my limbs as I went. He slammed shut the wire door and I stopped laughing. Slowly I started to come down. I was sore. Loser disappeared into the bathroom, leaving me to stare at the dog through the crate. *The dog is out, and I am in. The dog is out, and I am in.*

I started to shake. I rattled the bars of the cage, 'I need the loo!' I screamed. No answer. I urinated. I was left sitting in a pool of my own concentrated piss.

I had been trapped inside the crate for so long now, I couldn't hold my shit in any longer. I had no choice but to defecate in front of Loser, who had wandered back in. He lay on the floor and watched closely as my orifice opened. Steam rose as it slopped out on to the floor. He was laughing, loving my degradation.

I tried to squash it through the bars, leaving warm shit on the base of my foot. Claustrophobic and dirty, I had cramp. I was cold. I had cloudy eyes as my contacts needed cleaning. I blinked uncontrollably, tapped my foot a thousand times and scratched myself till I bled. I heard noises in other rooms, pipes clanking, murmuring of voices, music. Sting's smooth tones on the radio.

Loser eventually opened the door of the crate, scooped up a smattering of shit and spread it over my belly. It stank, but it didn't stop his erection. He stood up, closed his eyes and breathed deeply. He lathered the remainder on to his balls and started wanking, occasionally opening his eyes to peer at me through the crate, checking that I was still there. He stopped just before he came and dragged me to the shower. He turned on the freezing cold water and I screamed with shock as he pushed me under. He changed the temperature, kicked me out of the way and got in himself.

He stepped out, dried, and calmly picked up the dog's collar and lead from a chair. He placed it around my neck and buckled it up. How many holes? One, two, three. *Mum, can you hear me? Dad, are you there?*

I had no choice but to follow him. He was erect again. He yanked the lead, I choked. He pulled me up on to the bed and ripped into my hole hard, big slamming strokes that made the bed move an inch every time. He held on to the lead, pulling tighter and tighter.

Dear God, is it my time?

Laughing, laughing, laughing. Loser made a habit of putting me in that stinking crate and shutting the door. I did not fight, I did not whimper, I did not moan, because this was not the first time, I knew he would be back. It was a sex game. I'd got used to it, just as his dog had got used to the crate.

Crate Training.
Place a puppy in a wire crate and lock the door. She will gnaw, whine, bark, but it won't be long before she is defeated. Silent, submissive, staring, waiting for her owner's return. Eventually, the puppy will go into the crate quite happily, wagging her tail as she goes. The crate is her comfort zone, her security, her home.

The wave
August 1992

I can't hear a song from the eighties on the radio without thinking of Matthew. B&Bs, hair in plaits, chocolate fingers. For me, a chocolate bar is no longer innocent. I see it as abuse and feel sick. I go down a big black hole inside my head. I desperately try to think of something else, anything, to claw my way out of the dark.

A kind of cloud arrives. I am cold and it is evil. Taking over my body, it demands, 'Why not now? Go kill yourself *now*. Go to that drawer and pick up that knife. That's it. Cut your wrist, now the other. Go on. In death you will be happy.'

Stop it! Go away! I am in despair. The cloud devours me, I am paralysed. Afraid to tell a soul, to be told I need medication. I dread the words, 'You have turned into your mother.' *But I can't have, a doctor once told me I was very lucid.*

I disappear for days under my covers, stinking. I can't eat but I drink vodka and snort whatever I can lay my hands on until the mist subsides.

I arrive back on top form with no explanation. I'm called elusive by my men. I call it a wave of depression.

I am not the greatest shagger I used to be. Not quite as loose, a little more raw. My emotions are closer to the surface. Thankfully no man notices the odd tear trickling down my cheek. They mistake my tense body as a not-wanting-sex game. They hold me down and drive into me harder. The more I struggle the more turned on they get. But I quickly remember how to fuck like a doll and let them do whatever they want. The only way I can get through it is by shutting myself down. If I don't, I'd probably never fuck again and that would be a disaster. *I have to get back to the old me. You're being too much of a sissy, snap out of it!*

But I couldn't. My dark cloud returned, and frequently; it interrupted my ability to perform. I went from loving sex to hating sex, to feeling empty when I'd had sex, to dreading sex, to needing to be drunk to have sex. Bribed to have sex. To hurting people.

This is what happens to the sexually abused, they are sexually confused. Guilty, irrational, happy, sad. Loving, loathing, fearing, wanting. Maybe I should see a therapist? I can't, they'll get turned on by my exploits and end up wanking. Perverts. Therapy is for narcissists. Having the time to think about your feelings, to contemplate life, is a middle-class luxury. The therapist will bleed me dry and make me cry. Not a good idea. I won't be self-indulgent, I'll just get on with it, I am made of tougher stuff. I will wrap my past in a box and post it with no return to sender. The glass must always be half full. *There's always a child worse off than me.* Right, back on track. The power of talking to myself has saved me a fortune.

And when I stab my hand with my keys, dig my comb in my head, burn my scalp with my hair dryer and scratch my cunt until it's raw, I wonder if I do these things because I've not had therapy?

Dear God, where are you? I can't bear it, I don't want to be me any more. It's so draining being in my head. I'd like to be in someone else's, thinking of butterflies and fairies, flowers and fluffy kittens. Can I be in Yours? I just want to forget. Please, give me lithium, anything, a lobotomy.

Uncooked sausages

I have to tell someone what happened to me, for my own sanity. I am dry, my body is crying out for help. I need to face my enemy. I am ready.

I was shown to a squashy sofa in a room full of cuddly toys. It was just like my friend's mum's sitting room. The heat was on high, I knew I was red in the face. I took my cardy off. 'Please may I have a drink?' I asked with private school politeness to the counsellor woman who sat watching me.

I was nervous, I could feel myself shake as I spoke.

'The social worker liked to put things up my, you know,' I told her. 'He had these long nails. It hurt. He put his dick in my mouth, it was messy. I didn't like things being done to me at first. Problem is, that's a lie, because at first, I did want him to do things to me, or I thought I did. I encouraged him. After that, I cried every time he did it to me, I don't know why. It didn't make him stop. He liked me crying, it turned him on, made him go faster. Through my tears I liked it, but then I didn't. I was confused. I still am.

'I got presents in return, really nice ones. He threw an Argos catalogue at me, telling me to choose something, anything. It became routine. I thought of each new gift while he did it. I always thought of other things while he did it. He was true to his word, the gifts would arrive, but then I would always have to say "Thank you." So then it started all over again. I got so used to it all after a while, he didn't have to ask. Then I made him do things to me. He took me to places, to his house, motels. These days, sometimes I still cry after sex, I don't know why.'

The counsellor woman listened with no outward emotion. *Blimey, she must have been in this job a long time.*

'I used to keep saying a phrase to myself,' I continued, 'over and over: "There's always a child worse off than me." And it's true, there is, isn't there? I mean, I wasn't starving, or dying, was I? I wasn't in a Third World country. I was in England and in England we look after our children. We house them, feed them, keep them alive. How could I expect not to be, you know, "messed" with as well? It was attention. In my stupid immature child-like way, I loved him. Now of course I loathe him. Erotic moments with him have turned into horrific memories. Matthew was one bad egg, among so many good. The other workers at the home were so lovely, the cook and the cleaner, so warm. The other social workers gave me attention too, but it wasn't enough, not the attention I wanted, not the attention I liked. I wanted to be messed with. Matthew messing with me was love. I'm fucked in the head because I liked it when I knew I shouldn't. I think I am bitter because my life might have repaired itself, if Matthew had been a good egg. Now I fear he is out there, under the radar, free to reoffend. Mess with others.'

Bitch fuck woman hasn't even raised an eyebrow.

'It was my fault. I think I know why Matthew went for me, it was because I had a knowing look, a dirty type of look, a sort of inappropriate longing that you see in grown-ups' eyes, not in children's. I was easy prey because my cunt was prepped. My innocence gone because I'd already been spoiled.'

The counsellor woman shifted in her seat. Her skirt was stuck to her thighs. She had those see-through tights on that made her legs look like uncooked sausages. *Bet your tights make you sweat! I imagine you're itchy too, itchy to go on your lunch break, you look bored stiff. Heard it all before no doubt, 'Same old, same old' is it? It's not to me. You could at least show some compassion. This meeting may mean nothing to you, but it means everything to me.*

She blinked, twice. She was human after all, or maybe a hair was in her eyes.

'It is never a child's fault,' she said finally. 'It was grooming.'

She can speak.

I interrupted her and replied, 'Technically it may have been grooming, but it felt like being seduced to me.'

She ignored my comment and went on, 'Then it was rape, and it was wrong.'

She could see my facade was breaking, at last so was hers. *No, I can't do nice. Please don't be nice or I'll cry. I need to be hard-boiled. No one must crack open my shell, ever get to my core.*

'I really struggle with the word "rape",' I replied. 'You may call me a rape victim, but I don't really see myself as one. I longed for him, I took pleasure from this "rape". I don't feel what I imagine a rape victim to feel. I mean, it wasn't some stranger down an alleyway, I *knew* him. That's not rape. Is it?'

'You were a minor, he was an adult. He sexually abused you. It is irrelevant that you may have eventually, as you put it, "wanted" it. He made you "want" it. He groomed you.'

'I hear what you are saying, but after a while it didn't feel wrong.'

'After a while?' she repeated. Cocking her thin brow, which I suspected was pencilled in.

'What am I saying? Not, "after a while", not at all. You are forgetting I wasn't pure.'

'All the more reason to protect you,' she replied.

I giggled inappropriately and scratched my arm, unaware I was breaking the skin.

'It sounds like you're protecting him,' she added.

Such a mind fuck to get my head around. I jumped up and announced, 'I need the loo.'

Scrubbing my hands, I looked in the mirror and said to my reflection, 'You were raped.' *How embarrassing.*

'You were *raped!*' I shouted at myself.

'No, I wasn't, I had sex with Matthew because I wanted to.'

'No, you didn't.'

'Yes I did. I was gagging for it!'

'He ripped your knickers off remember, you were shy, you put your hand over your mouth and said "No, I don't want to." Remember?'

'Yes, but I liked it really.'

'No, you didn't.'

'Yes I did. It was attention. Distraction. Love!'

'You can call it what you like, but it was rape.'

'No, it wasn't.'

'Yes, it was rape, rape, *rape!*'

I punched the glass.

I am arguing with my own reflection, I must be off my rocker, turning into my mother again. This burning shame and fury welling, where has it come from? Am I finally connecting with my emotions? Suffering, because that's what rape victims are supposed to do? I have to face up to the shame that I liked it. How did Matthew turn my brain like that? Is that normal? I have lost the sense of right and wrong. I must retrain my brain.

I looked in the mirror one last time and saw a child staring back at me screaming.

'You need to go away,' I said.

The child in me replied, 'I won't go till you're *dead!*'

Upon re-entering the sweltering room, I said: 'Children only know what you show them. Being abused seemed sort of normal to me at the time.'

'*Why* didn't you tell?' my counsellor couldn't help but blast. I looked down at the floor. 'Call Childline?' she roared. I swung my foot. 'It was set up for children, just like you.'

I looked up at her. 'It didn't exist then,' I whispered. *And by the time it had I was into white socks and Vaseline.*

'Why didn't you tell anyone at the time?' she repeated.

Matthew is a shadow that I cannot cast off. How can you ever begin to understand? I am still a child in fear of a shadow, a shadow that will only dissipate in death. It took courage for me to see you today, courage I didn't have back then. Your lot would have taken him from me.

My counsellor explained to me that the more sexually abused a child is, the more compensation they receive. She proceeded to read out a file that contained matter-of-fact accounts of what had happened to victims and how much they had been awarded in recompense. That haunting list hounded me at night. I wish I'd never listened.

If a girl was raped at 12 years old, she'd be buying a car with the proceeds. If she was six, she'd be putting a deposit on a flat.

I received nothing. I felt strongly about not wanting to be paid for shagging a paedophile; it was ironic, seeing as Matthew had paid me anyway. It just didn't feel right. According to that list, I could have been driving around in a brand-new Mini. I could park outside school gates and shout from a tannoy, 'If a bad man has stuck it in your private parts, you can have a car for free, with taxpayers' money!' I think I was missing the point.

The funny thing was, Matthew had offered to buy me a Mini himself. In red. I'd have preferred a black one, but I guess red would do.

I wanted Matthew to be tried in a Crown Court and be sent to prison for his crime. But a solicitor informed me that all I could do was sue him for damages, 'Too much time has elapsed,' they said. It was only my word against his.

Damages. That meant money. What about justice? I wanted him to pay time, not money, for what he had done. No one told me I could demand an inquiry of children's homes in the borough.

The police told me that Matthew had, when questioned, said that he wanted to represent himself. So I'd have had to face him in court, only a few feet away. Relive those sex acts all over again with him listening, staring, his dick straining, enjoying me.

'Can't I go behind a screen or something?' I asked anxiously.

I could imagine him saying to the police, 'But she asked for it. She came to my room and asked for it.'

Matthew, this is true. We both know that after a bit, I did. But that's not the point. I was a child, remember?

He rang me when he shouldn't. Down the phone he was angry. 'I'll get you!' he threatened. His words plagued me. *I don't want to live here any more.*

Creamy custard
November 1992

Why would some tosser want to do over a poor girl's council flat? They must have been desperate. Or was the burglary connected to Matthew? He had, after all, put in new locks for me when I'd moved in. Had he kept a set of keys?

The burglar had gone through *everything*. Taken anything that might be worth something, including my scruffy old diary that I had written in an illegible scrawl in at the kids' home. And all my money. Shame, I was a cash girl, and I had *a lot*.

I could feel the thief's presence in my underwear drawer, his hands rifling through. God, I felt vulnerable. I ran back to my mum and dad for a hug. *I smell lunch in the oven as I walk through the door. Kitty meows at my feet. The sound of cartoons and giggles of younger siblings. The muffled laughter of Dad. The drone of a vacuum cleaner with Mum humming away, making my old bedroom nice for me to stay in till I feel better. Dad says he'll do a bit of DIY to get my flat looking shipshape again: 'I'll change the locks for you too. You'll feel safe then.'*

Of course I was daydreaming. I was alone with a longing that would never come true. *Where are you, Dad?* Staring at my clothes strewn all over the floor and at the empty space where my money once lay, I cried and screamed with rage about the family that didn't belong to me and the sucking of some fat man's balls so I could eat tonight.

I strode past my mum's, looked up and saw the light was on. Was she singing? I wish she was baking, that's what normal mums do. I whizzed up the stairs and knocked on her door.

She didn't answer.

'I've been burgled, Mum,' I shouted. '*Burgled*. Can you believe it? They took everything, bar my parka.'

She didn't answer. A waste of time, I was talking to her door again.

I stood still and listened for a moment.

'*Hey Mr Tambourine Man...*'

At least she was alive. I sang along for a second, then left.

I stood outside a lap dancing club knowing some man would come out with a hard-on, that is if he hadn't discharged already.

Lying there in an old prune's flat, I felt one tentative lick, then another, more confident this time.

'That's it, old boy, that's it!' Then prune face went for it, big time. He spread me wide open and dived in.

Prune, I want to hurt you, smother you, drown you in my juices, leave you lifeless, you old wanker. But I've been burgled, I need the money.

Seeing the back of his dandruffy head moving about made me want to smack it. His horrid hairy back, his flat white arse.

I want to vomit in your mouth.

Just as well I can detach myself from a situation, I thought, as I worked out what I'd buy in Tesco's later with his cash. *Boil-in-the-can treacle tart, yes, love that. Can of creamy custard too, served cold. Mmm.*

'Do you like my meaty sausage?' Prune asked. 'It comes with two juicy veg.' *Jesus, this one's been watching too much Benny Hill.*

Stab, stab, stab. *Have I got a tin opener? I did have or did the bastard burglar take that as well?*

He withdrew and demanded, 'Eat your meat!' *I'll buy biscuits, buttery ones, to dip in my milky tea. Do I have any tea left?*

'Gobble me up, baby. Lick my dick like it's your favourite ice cream.' *Jesus, the crap he's coming out with.*

Lick, lick, lick. I didn't really mind. When I was low I liked it. *I wonder if I can get a fresh bloomer at this time of night? So warm and squidgy, yum.*

'Now I'm going to make you gag!' he cried. He all but choked me, jamming his dick hard into my tonsils. Then pulled it out with a flourish. *Yuck! Don't come on my hair. Now I'll have to put an extra tenner on my charge key for the gas meter, to wash my bloody hair.*

'Another tenner till next time pleeeease?' I pleaded, with my head cocked and a big grin. Prune seemed to be a sucker for it, though. I thought he might pay up and that would be that. But:

'I'm not finished yet,' he said.

I am. I'm hungry. What d'you want to do now?

Prune tied me up with the belt from his dressing gown. My tummy was rumbling. *Rumble, rumble, rumble in the jungle.*

He covered my face with the gown. *Rank,* I thought, as I lay there face down on his bed. *It needs a wash.*

He went to put the kettle on. Then some other man came in.

I see.

This stranger, his smell, his touch, his taste... so greedy. Prune turned up the radio so the neighbours couldn't hear me. I learnt long ago that if I struggled less, and embraced abuse, I'd not bruise. I gave in and offered myself willingly.

Mum, don't you think I'm worth at least another tenner? I think I should ask for more.

The stranger stopped and turned to Prune who had come back in to watch. I struggled free. *Please! Leave me be! I want to go home and eat treacle tart.*

But I was not allowed.

February 1993

My court case never ended. In the meantime, Matthew went to prison for some other offence. I couldn't find out what crime he'd committed or the length of his sentence. 'Fuck another child did he?' I asked. 'That's confidential,' my lawyer said. 'He has a right to privacy. If he wanted you to know of his crime he would tell you himself.'

I could have waited until his release and continued, as I had free legal aid because I had a strong case. But I felt as if I couldn't move on. I was anxious, I couldn't sleep. I was nervous of him, how I'd cope in court. By the way I was grilled by the lawyers, it felt as if I was the perpetrator. It was draining having endless meetings with second-rate solicitors in the suburbs.

'We just wanted to keep you up to date,' my lawyer droned, looking at my fat file. I swear I could see cobwebs. 'There's nothing to inform you of right now,' she added. *Pen pusher!*

I was believed by many and doubted by few; I had won anyway.

'I want to close the case,' I told her eventually.

She was shocked. 'Are you sure?'

'Very!'

The educated classes
June 1994

Who cares if I gorged on a clever student's cock in return for a little help with punctuation for my final dissertation? I got my degree. I gave no blow jobs to the lecturers for a few extra marks. I wouldn't have minded, all that grey hair got me going.

I was now out of the gutter. I was skilled, educated and not dead. My achievements were small to the accomplished, but huge to me. Not bad for a cunt with fake pearls. I'd fucked my way out. I was proud. I ran to my mum's.

'Mum, Mum, open the door! I got a degree. Little me got a degree.'

I was talking to her door again, wish she'd open it, I'd like to see her smile at my news, even if it is a snarling, gnashing, dog-type smile.

'I got a really high mark!' I shouted through the letterbox. She didn't answer. I left and told the good news to a lady in the launderette instead. She wasn't really listening. Why should she? She didn't know me. I don't think she understood English either, but that's not the point, it was just nice to say it out loud.

'I got a degree.'

I miss talking to you, Mum. You know we've never had that.

Masala dosa

I think I'll be freelance, not that I'll ever earn any money from my 'job', I rely on men for that. I am a cunt for sale who hides it well, who needs a front so people don't ask too many questions about how I'm sometimes dripping with cash. Maybe I'll travel first, a smart man likes a woman who has travelled. I could then tell a smart man I'd been on a gap year. That would be a language he'd understand.

I needed a cushion to get me started. I was offered seven grand as a start up, by an entrepreneur I met in a private members' club. After a few flirty chats, I realised that all that was required was a blow job. He had his driver waiting outside with the engine still running. The dirty git wouldn't sign the cheque till I swallowed. Silly man, I'd have done it for £70. *When did I start being this vile? I want to be nice again.*

I fucked off and backpacked with my wallet taped to my leg, passport down my knickers, zero jewellery, 90 contact lenses and the *Lonely Planet* as my bible. I had no fear, wasn't green around the ears and thought I didn't give a damn about dying, a hard girl abroad.

I loved the anonymity of travelling. The weight of my social status lifted, I was classless, no one judged me, I was anything, I was free. I avoided the English on holiday, they annoyed me, reminding me of Matthew and the taste of him I'd left behind. Never mind my mad mother, she was a constant worry, it was like I'd left the bath running or something.

Life wasn't that bad. At least when I was mugged by a man of authority on the other side of the world I wasn't raped too. Always glass half full me.

'Merry Christmas, God bless you!' I said when he fleeced me. *Arsehole!*

That little incident did not put me off travelling on through Peru, Columbia, Bolivia, Paraguay, Brazil. To Guinea-Bissau, Togo, Oman, Russia, China. To a rumble, rumble, rumble from an earthquake in a gun village in Pakistan. Nearly knocked my hat off and blew my cover, I was disguised as a boy. They had these amazing Bond-style gun pens for sale; I should have shoved one up my arse, flown it home and shot Matthew. India. The cleaners wouldn't make eye contact, apparently deemed unworthy. If they'd known what they were looking at, they wouldn't have wanted to anyway. But a homeless girl did, she looked at me with longing to follow me home. *There's always a child worse off than me.*

When my travels were over, my body was heavy. I was back in misery with two pints of pus and a burst appendix. I came off the plane dying and the doctors didn't know why, until they opened me up. I lost a lot of weight, but that was a good thing, I was one big masala dosa when it happened.

Drips in my arm, bruises from my veins collapsing and the nurse trying again and again to fit a needle in my arm.

'A baby needle, *please*,' I roared.

'How were your travels?' the nurse enquired, trying to distract me. I found them hard to describe; being educated did not make me eloquent. 'Go and see for yourself,' I replied.

A frumpy-looking female doctor swished in, flopped on to my chair and frowned, 'There were complications, you might not be able to have children,' she said. *Why did you tell me that? Now I won't be able to have children because I'll be worried about not being able to have children. Bitch.* I wouldn't allow this information to sink in, or think of the baby I'd flushed down the loo – perhaps the only baby I'd ever have. *Dear God, I want a child and you will NOT be this cruel! I will have a child, I will, I will, I WILL!*

Seven beds full and me, the youngest in the hospital ward. All that was left of me was skin and bone and my blood was slowly poisoning me from septicaemia. I fell asleep to the sound of girls having fun on the Fulham Road.

I went to heaven and back. Rising over my bed towards cumulus clouds, those cute fluffy white ones that Uncle Danny had once tasted. A force pushing me, then weightlessness. I looked down and saw myself unaware. I was at peace, in some nasty night gown, not my colour. *Hang on, no. I don't want to die just yet.*

Whoosh! I fell back into my body and woke with a start.

Did that really happen? That was uncomfortably close. I do not like death, far too final. How can people just be gone? But death is the most natural thing in the world, and I am going to die whether I want to or not, how annoying. I don't want the choice of the date of my death taken from me, I want to go when I decide. The good thing about it, though, is that I won't know I am dead. I won't know the difference; I'll probably think I'm asleep. I forgot, I won't be thinking at all.

Seeing as I was almost there, I decided to organise my own funeral in case I did die. The songs I'd have, who was going to be invited and who definitely wasn't. My family, for starters. And I would be buried with a non-religious spokesperson leading the service.

The reading
Be happy for me, for I will be gone. This is what I want, for I will be free. Yet let me stay with thee, my ego couldn't take being forgotten.

The epitaph

'She scathed the world and loathed most humans, but very much loved her own.'

Shame they didn't love me back.

The flowers

Lilies. Convenient, considering they are a sign of death. Roses would not have been quite so appropriate.

But what do I care about appropriate? Ignored in life, fawned on in death, that will be me. The relatives will come out of the woodwork. 'Did she leave anything for me?' *Scavengers! No more crying, my little magpies, I am glad to be dead.*

They'll be crying for all the wrong reasons, of course. It won't be for my skin and bone, sunken eyes and the long slit of what was once my mouth lying there, in the overpriced, velvet-lined coffin with big brass bits that they've ordered so as to not look tight. Along with the two stretch limos seeing as I'm only going to die the once. Hoping the other will pay. Such a waste of money, if I had known about it I'd have said to them, 'Forget the funeral, I'm just meat waiting to be disposed of. Throw me away in nothing but vintage Biba. Save the coffin for some other death some other day.'

'I'll so miss her!' they'll say, as Kate Bush plays 'Room For The Life'. Selfish pigs, no they won't. My death will get in the way of their routine. They'll feel awkward trying to act subdued. I know I would. It's difficult for me to keep a straight face at a funeral as a belly laugh is bursting to come out. I have what is called 'displaced emotion'. It's a defence mechanism, more like a madness.

Maybe I'll change my request to cremation. I don't like the thought of all those insects with a thousand legs boring into me, thriving on my rancid flesh. I'm a murdering bitch so they'd probably not go near me.

I was at that big old hospital for over five weeks with not one family visitor, apart from my mum, but she didn't count. All she did was scrub stains from the high-backed hospital chairs and pace up and down, eyes wild and mumbling. *Give it a rest, Mum.*

I asked the nurse to draw the curtains around my bed so I wouldn't have to look at her, as she interacted with the others in the ward.

'Yuck, you smell,' she jeered to the pensioner in the bed opposite. 'You've messed yourself!' The lady was so tiny, all you could see of her were the blankets. 'Ugh!' Mum went on, loudly, to no one in particular, 'she's messed herself. Smelly pants. Smelly, smelly, smelly pants.' Bless her, Mum was only saying what the rest of us were thinking.

She attacked another patient who had a slight weight problem. 'You're so fat and ugly,' she cried. 'You look like a beached whale. Fat, fat, *fat*!' My mum could hardly talk, she was a fat fucker herself, from fry ups and comfort eating. Sixteen stone of blubber on a small-boned woman was a lot. *Nurse, get my heifer of a mother out of here!*

'Fa-a-t!' she shouted. 'She must be here to staple her stomach,' she went on. 'You look like a cunt,' she hissed. That was it. I tried to explain her illness to the nurses, but they banned her.

Unsuccessfully, as she crept back into the ward, stark naked and giggling.

'She only wants to use the shower,' I told the nurse, laughing to myself, watching Mum's blobby unclothed body running away from security.

'Now you be getting away from me-e-e-e-e!'

I was crawling the walls. I started thinking about Matthew. He would have come to see me; brought me a magazine and some Rolos. I'd have enjoyed watching his sad face as I ate the last one, then made him happy by saying, 'Come visit tomorrow!' only so I could get some more. I shuffled to the canteen with my temporary colostomy bag in full view and sat down beside a visitor eating marble cake. I slapped my bowel contents on to the Formica table top for amusement and watched while the visitor retched.

I think it's time to go home. I begged the doctors to release me. 'If not I'll be discharging myself.'

It took me weeks to get my strength back. I was loath to claim benefits. From my bed, I absorbed Radiohead and watched life go by in my street, fixating on my new, well-to-do neighbour.

She moved in with the help of Cadogan Tate and fit boys in Ts. A piano, a leather sofa, lots of mirrors, a huge glass table. Why have you decided to live here? D'you think it's cool to live among the likes of me?

'Notting Hill, so raw, so real, so cool, yet so quaint at the same time,' I overhear you say in a breathy voice to a fellow clone.

'Quaint', what does that mean? Do you love the romanticism of the dilapidated buildings with their peeling paint being sold for a song? The scruffy shops and the no-go streets like All Saints Road? Hard drugs, deals in shop doorways, desperation?

Locals were savvy, outsiders naive, the criminals, waiting. If you were known, they'd leave you alone.

So many parking spaces, so few cars. The police always on stand-by for the next raid. Kids high from sweets tore round the Tabernacle, terrorising old folk, spoiling the only haven for the community. Westbourne Grove, such a graveyard, only frequented for a stamp or a shit, nothing else there. Time for Carnival. The smell of spliff, the music so free. Dearest neighbour, you're too late for 'quaint', that description was of 1978.

I'm none too pleased, neighbour, you're playing at being someone like me. Acting all street, dropping your Ts and spitting out your plum till you go back to your childhood home for Christmas. I do not have that luxury.

Have you ever thought about the consequences of you living here? Constantly reminding people like me that I have fuck all when you park your shiny new car in a space that should house my non-existent one. My flat is the size of your kitchen, your house is the size of my block.

Through my window I see you hold parties. Toffs spill champagne while dancing, laughing as food falls to the floor. I'm hungry again. I'm also chippy. All these new cafes and bakeries round here cater for you, not me. I walk past one, two, three, four, five of them before finding one I can go into without security stalking me. Resentment is building, dear neighbour.

'But look at what my kind has done to your area!' you exclaim. 'Why complain when we've smartened it up?'

You're so imperceptive, you need an education. Who am I, I am poor, I live in a council flat. I can't afford to live in my own area any more, but I cannot leave when I like. I am trapped. I do not have the freedom to move to a different postcode, that would take money, and I have none.

The cheap supermarket has gone, instead stands an Organic Food Emporium. The local charity shop is gone, a designer store is opening. That's no good for me, is it?

My much-needed pound shop has gone. Can't you feel my bitterness? The uneasy atmosphere of poor against rich? You don't notice it because you don't want to notice it. You don't mix with the locals, the real deals like me. You hang out with your own. They are your neighbours, not me. I've brushed past your kind for years, but you don't see me.

I wish you'd thought it through before moving into my area. I now can't enjoy it because you're in it. I wished you'd fuck off back to Kensington or Chelsea,

I don't want to see you tottering by on expensive high heels, hailing a cab I can never afford.

And don't you dare look right through me. Or worse, step away when I slope past you, drooling over your Chanel handbag. It's only luck that you are not me. Life and where you're placed, pure chance.

Don't apologise, be more discreet, because when I see you looking smug with your designer shopping, I just want to rip it from your arm. I see you, dear neighbour, I see it all. I want to be you, I will be you one day.

Be careful how you treat others, your behaviour may come back to haunt you. Do not be surprised when a brick gets thrown through your window, your door is graffitied and your bag is snatched from your arm. You chose to live here, what did you expect? A street party with the salt of the earth welcoming you? Offering to wash your smalls and tend your garden? It's your fault. You came north of Kensington for more floor space and a bit of grit, I'm afraid you have to take what comes with the territory.

Feeling vulnerable from the mugging, I bet you wish you still lived in your apartment in Chelsea, you greedy patronising Sloane. I bring you a yummy cake and coo over your 'frightening' experience. While I'm here, dear neighbour, take a good look at my new handbag. It was bought with the proceeds of selling yours on the estate.

Millennium
New Year 2000

I was fighting fit, educated, well travelled and with coke up my fanny, I met a Big Player and had a mad time. I thought the white stuff inhibited a man's libido, at times Matthew couldn't even get it up, but there was no flaccid member on this man. I screamed from the rooftops with orgasm after orgasm. He was pure animal, the room a wreck. I was infatuated. He took me across the Channel to a cottage in the country. With Bob Dylan blaring, we knew every line, and we partied hard. Spliffed to the eyeballs, I later passed out and threw up in my sleep, missing the turn of the millennium. The next thing I knew was him jumping into bed naked, landing slap bang in my sick. Not a way to endear myself, especially when there was no hot water to wash himself down with. He dumped me soon after that. Bereft I was, but not surprised.

At least I could shag him, pure chemistry I suppose. Strangely, I didn't want to lacerate him, I felt we were sort of equal. My cunt was always open for a salacious fuck if he fancied it, sucking him was easy, he was so obscene; I'd have licked his piss from a toilet bowl, but not with the next man, his requests were too weird.

'Ah, ah, not allowed to touch!' I said to the Eurotrash I'd picked up in Knightsbridge. I had big tits from gel chicken fillets in my bra. I pushed his hand away in case he knocked my silicone helpers out of place. I let his fingers tiptoe up the inside of my leg and over my stockings. I had no pubic hair, so he glided in easily with his thumb. I like thumbs, I gently rocked against it.

'Will you nurse me?' he asked. *I don't think so. Too out there*. Instead, I dozed with his spent dick in my mouth, while he gently molested me. I found it soothing. He didn't seem to mind. He stared lustfully at my tits, and proceeded to tell me he was breast fed till he was five. 'I remember it clearly,' he sighed. He'd have been very disappointed to see me without my clothes on.

I finally had the money, it was time for the op. I loved the quizzical looks I saw on old mates' faces when they glanced at my new breasts and wondered to themselves, *Has she had a tit job?* Yes I have, but I'm not going to tell you about the plastic surgeon whom I paid to mutilate my horrible tits, who pulled them open and placed a foreign body under my muscle with the huge potential of infection and rejection. I woke up with tubes inserted into my breasts, enjoying the discomfort. *It'll be so worth it*, I thought.

The next day I looked in the mirror and through the fog of Tramadol, I smiled to myself. Through the bandages I could see they were bigger. A fantastic pair of glorious new titties, best thing I ever did. With the power of my new pillows, my cunt saw far less usage. All a man wanted to do now was bury his face in them, dribble spit on my nipples and bite.

I felt I was now all woman. I wanted to get away from the skinny powerless me. I was moving from the men who like their lovers to look like children, who want control, to the men who like their women to look like mothers: soft, fleshy, wholesome. Men who get off on women having control, much more healthy.

It was important for me to look good. Weekly blow-dries paid for by daily blow jobs. The odd facial, a manicure. Lots of make-up and no knickers. In the mirror I noticed frown lines. *Shit!* Was that from all the frowning while concentrating on my studies? Or from sucking cock? I've got to get rid of these wrinkles otherwise no man will want me. I have to look pretty, open, available. I don't know how to exist without a man. Wrinkles frighten me, I have not bagged a husband yet.

I so wanted a husband who would look after me. But how would I find him? He had to be rich; I refused to be poor. If I were a model it would be easy, men would just fall in love with my beauty. But I'm not a model, I'll have to work harder.

I was a great believer in family, in children, a unit. I hadn't had that myself, yet it was such a powerful desire. *Family*, the very word made me want to puke, but I contradicted myself by wanting one of my own. And I didn't want my children to come from a deprived or dysfunctional family. I'd have a proper husband and give them a stable upbringing. Then there would be more chance that they'd end up being normal, whatever that meant.

C & E

Rock 'n' roll families, crazy messy families, so bohemian, so overrated. Lucky are the children who grow up in a normal environment. Tidy, ordered, clean.

A cat, a nice squashy sofa, a sitting room brimming with trinkets. A mum who is a school secretary; a dad, a cashier at the bank. Rules and regulations, meals at the same time every day. School shirts ironed, skirts clean, bedrooms tidy. Their toys placed neatly in labelled boxes, their lives perfect. Such houses breathe boredom, but are a secret longing for me, who was raised in clutter and chaos. Normal people are my favourite now. No game playing, no agenda, no tricks.

Their clothes are always safe, good quality over fashion, from a brand they can trust. They never drink except on a special occasion. Drugs never enter their stratosphere. They always read *The Times* and eat nothing but fish on a Friday. Religion? 'Only C & E', Christmas and Easter, relief.

Dear Normal Person, will you be my best friend? You represent solid values and I crave that.

I surprise my old mates with a refusal of a binge as I'm off for afternoon tea in the world's safest car with my nice normal friend.

Hanging out with normal people didn't last long. When I was passed a slice of drizzle cake I just wanted to say, 'Yuck! Cunt juices!' Not, 'Why, thank you.'

I found it all too tedious. I had to behave all the time, I couldn't even fucking swear. Anyway, I might as well dump them before they dumped me. They wouldn't want to know me once they'd found out I wasn't from a nice normal family.

But where did this idea of wanting to have a family of my own come from? I know where, from killing a baby. Maybe if that hadn't happened, I wouldn't have had this yearning to correct my wrongdoing.

I will have children. I will, I will, I will! I must repeat what I want and it will happen. *See that baby's hand and I will come. Hear that pitter patter and I will belong. Motherhood is calling me.*

Just not yet, I must get married first because I was brought up a Catholic, which instilled good values in me. I wouldn't be saying that out loud of course. I preach that it's a load of bollocks, especially the praying bit. And God, schmod, who made Him up? As if there really is some Superbeing watching over me. If He is, He's pretty elusive. How stupid does the Church think I am? There will be no wedding for me in a church, that's for sure.

I'll get married and have a fairy-tale ending to my life. I will, I will, I will.

I must repeat what I want and it will happen.

THREE

'Faith is the substance of things hoped for, the evidence of things not seen.'

HEBREWS 11:1

A confident man
October 2001

We were two dirty dogs whoring round town when we met each other, future husband and wife.

I had blagged my way into a members' bar and set eyes on this older, beautiful man, surrounded by four wanton women. I was not fazed by them; all is fair in love and war.

Most men wanted a classy girl on their arm, Josh wanted dirty and ever ready for his next feel. He saw my tits before he saw me, sheer blouse, no bra. He liked it. He moved the other women out of the way, came closer and sniffed. Unwashed fanny and expensive perfume. An acquired taste. He fucking loved it.

He climbed the stairs to my flat and declared it was 'quaint'. I chose to ignore that offensive remark. But when he commented on my wallpaper – 'just like my mother's' – I knew I was on to a good thing. Men are always looking for their mother in a wife.

If I want something I go get it, I never wait for it to come to me. His greying hair made me moist. I held his thumb and guided him in. 'What's this?' he said, feeling my bare cunt with disapproval. I knew then he was no paedophile. We shagged and the condom broke.

I had a good feeling about Josh, with his soft features and kind eyes he was unthreatening, he had 'gentle' written on his forehead, that was important to me. I was better to him than I'd been to most. I amazed myself by not wanting to hurt him, to spit in his tea when he wasn't looking.

Not knowing where it was going, I shagged others, so did he. I made sure I shut up when I shagged him though, I didn't want to put him off with my less than normal sex requests. Fisting him face down just didn't seem appropriate, weeing on him he wouldn't like.

We'd meet in the Jacuzzi at the members' club and make each other laugh with our stories of the previous night's exploits in explicit detail, while fondling each other under the foam. Then I'd dive in the pool, and slowly piss while doing the breaststroke. Smiling as I swam past an unsuspecting member who was oblivious to my actions. Josh and I saw each other more and I saw others less, a risk as they gave me money. When it came to whoring, I felt we were on the same level. He had met his match whether he liked it or not.

Josh asked me to escort him to some event out of town. 'Yes, but I don't do B&Bs,' I told him. *They remind me of the panic of being poor.*

I needn't have worried. He took me to a swanky hotel with two sinks in the bathroom. It was so grand, it didn't even have a kettle for a cuppa in the room. *Fuck me!* But I acted cool, like I'd been to so many. I had, but never a five star, that was a first.

When I was glammed up and ready, he took the lift, I took the stairs. I'm not keen on small spaces, not sure why. Same with loos, I'd rather piss myself than shut the door.

I scrubbed up well. The host presumed I was my man's hire for the night, I looked far too trophy to be his girlfriend. Girlfriends seem to make less of an effort than single girls on the whole. Not me.

Josh loved that my pungent smell was a magnet for others; they were all cave men after all. He marvelled at how I worked the room so quickly. *My darling, you don't know, but I am a pro, not that I'm ever EVER going to tell you that.* Just as well he was a confident man. He did not realise I was a skank.

Off I smooched with some wrinkly old fellow with false teeth. Clamping my body tight against his, he felt my breasts while I whispered to him, soothing his ego, encouraging his rising. I enticed him into the disabled loo after he had fondled my triangle without invitation. *How dare you! No dirty old man will feel me unless I want him to. No dirty old man will ever dominate me unless I want him to. I am empowered.*

I rubbed the old codger's crotch, unzipped his flies, took out his thing – which was surprisingly hard – and let him have a peek of me. His cane fell abruptly to the floor. I enjoyed watching him almost having a heart attack when he saw my flesh. It reminded me of many an old man gasping as they held me open, looking, so wanting to touch, before desire took over and they destroyed me.

Thrilled by being so close to my perfectly smooth cunt – a bone of contention between me and my new man – the old boy prematurely ejaculated. I humiliated him further by mocking his yucky limp member. His crumpled hands found it difficult to put away his manhood without his cane to steady him. Flustered, he tried to bend down to pick it up, but slipped to the floor. I laughed and stabbed his fingers with my stilettos on the way out.

Is this cruelty? He'll not be able to put his fingers up a little girl's fanny any more. Flirty old men will forever be paedophiles to me.

The lines are blurring, so confusing. I am becoming paranoid.

Butterflies
February 2002

My last tryst was a spectacular blowout of coke with a fair-weather friend and her husband. The musky smell of her fanny lingered on my nose next morning as I slid into the Jacuzzi beside Josh.

'Enough about her fanny,' he said, 'Did you shag her betrothed?'

Just as well I didn't. I found out I was pregnant two weeks later. I wouldn't have known whose it was. Josh was shocked but delighted. He told me he'd done his whoring. 'I'm ready,' he said. I'd half expected him to say: 'Let me take you away somewhere nice after a termination.'

I am a Catholic, when it suits me, so no abortion this time. The baby may not have been quite how I planned it, but not even flying first class would have changed my mind. *God, was this Your doing? I was told my insides were messed up. Thank you, thank you!*

For the first few days after that, I had great fun in seeking out ex-shags and, if they didn't know already, telling them my good news.

'I'm pregnant,' I gushed.

'Whose is it?' they blurted.

'Yours!' I teased. Their faces dropped in horror, before they realised I was joking.

One of them said, 'But you only gave me a blow job!' News spread across Ladbroke Grove and into the cafe where my fair-weather friend and her skinny husband were lounging. I got a nervous phone call from her. I was kind. 'No, it's not your husband's, darling, he never had the pleasure of my hole. He was rabid for it though.'

Josh's mother cried. The fact I was an Irish Catholic was the icing on the cake. I didn't really know which part she was excited about, the 'Irish' or the 'Catholic'. I presumed it was the Irish part. Back in the day my green blood had given me nothing but contempt. Almost a generation later I was celebrated. I'm not complaining. I used to be called 'cool' because I was poor.

'You were homeless? Cool. Hungry? Even cooler. In care? Wow, you are the coolest girl ever!' But what's so cool about being in care? I don't get it. When you're in it, there's nothing 'cool' about it at all. Don't elevate adversity, celebrate misfortune, being poor is only cool to people who haven't been poor themselves. I don't ever remember having the conversation, 'We are so cool!' to other kids at the home. More like, 'Sisters and brothers, we are fucked!' There is nothing cool about eating from a bin.

Still fucking others while pregnant. Why not? It's a fetish I can get paid loads of money for. I could be in one of those magazines, I'm very neat down there. I'll fuck till it kicks or until I can at least feel the butterflies. I'm looking forward to feeling the butterflies. I'm already hankering for cheese.

The baby doesn't seem real yet anyway. The amount of coke I snorted before I knew I was pregnant, I'm surprised it's still here.

I was very careful about the coke now though. However much I pined for it when I was on a downer, seeing a dark cloud. I stopped myself reaching for the vodka. I pinched till I bruised and the moment passed.

Control, I had to be in control. I'd seen too many with damaged babies. Spliffing through pregnancies, delivering premature, underweight offspring. Babies housed in incubators until weaned off weed. Thick as fuck and always behind, what adult life would they lead?

My baby was due around Christmas. I was scared, bad things always happened to me at Christmas. I was worried I would have to face the wrath of God, He'd punish me for my sins, I'd give birth to a dead baby.

Dear God,

Men may hurt me, and I may have hurt others, but please don't give me a dead baby. Don't take it away, I am very much alive, I have been saved. I have risen, have You not noticed?

Apparently You will 'forgive us our trespasses' and for that, I will repent of my sins. This will be my day of atonement. Make me completely deaf, make me blind, but don't take my baby. Yes, I killed the last one, but my murdered baby up there in the candy floss clouds is allowing me a second chance. Can't You, God?

Come on, shine on me now, please help me. This is when I need You, need You to forgive me. I am begging You, God, see me now, notice me. Let my baby live long enough to walk through muddy puddles. Let me guide my child through Your love. Please?

No, I won't fuck others while pregnant but I so could. I'm not going to allow myself to love my fluttering foetus until I give birth and look down on its fully formed face and see it thriving.

'Mum, Mum! I'm having a baby! I know. Me!'

I don't know why I bother knocking, her door never opens. I'm going to paint it with eyes and a mouth soon, as I find myself chattering to it more than I'd like. I wonder if it's an 8 x 3 door or more of a 7 x 4. Is it hollow? Must be, it's council. The glass in it looks like it's about to crack. Crack up from laughing about me coming here to this hallway day after day, talking away at nothing but a chipped blue door and a bedraggled mop. Perhaps I'll draw a face on that too, it's already got great hair. Sometimes there's also a bag from Tesco's floating about.

'You looking for a bit of company? Here, come join us, there's always something going on at my mother's door. There was a cupboard here last week. You had to open the cupboard and climb right through it to knock on her door. The cupboard was broken of course, in bits it was. What she wanted to do with it, God knows. It being here sure was a fireman's dream. Health and safety are not high on my mother's list of priorities. Come to think of it, neither am I, judging by how little she answers the door.'

Tesco rustles beside me.

'If you can hear me,' I shout. 'Bye, Mum.'

I just wanted to tell you I am going to have a cot to fill and a kid to cuddle.

Nothing. Here's hoping.

I nod to the Tesco bag and leave. All of a sudden I have a yearning for brie.

My baby, if you're still alive next week and she hasn't burnt to death, I'll tell her about you then.

My mother's dream house
April 2002

'Janey mac, don't give it back!' my ragged uncle Danny begged. His big, scraggly beard had turned from red to white to yellow, with all the pipes he'd smoked.

I was a saint. I gave up my council flat to some other who was in need. I told Josh I'd given up a rental. He didn't need to know it was council. It had done its job, saving me from being stabbed in bed by my own mother. I could have kept it for ever, passed it on to my child, or illegally sublet it for four times its current rent on the open market, but that wouldn't have sat well with my Catholic conscience, especially as I was moving to Josh's house.

Uncle Bog threw himself at my feet. 'Give the flat to meeeee!'

So dramatic, the man had no shame. He clung on to my ankles like I was about to hand him over to the British or something. I shook him off like a rat up my trousers and sang, 'You're such a limpet, you should have been nice to me.'

My new home was practically the opposite, a serious bachelor pad. Flat-fronted with a wooden floor, high ceilings and intricate cornicing. I had moved into my mother's dream house. With heating in every room, a loo on every level and more than one TV. White, white, with everything designer, I'd stepped into an interiors magazine.

I soon got rid of the motorbike on the ground floor and replaced it with a Bill Amberg baby bag, a creamy sheepskin and a brand new Bugaboo to run over my scraggy uncle's feet with. *Piss off, you're embarrassing me!* Now I had a few pennies Uncle Danny was a cancer I couldn't rid of.

From council house to my own house. As I wake up I feel a gooey goose down pillow under my head, a mattress that moulds to my body. The warmth of under-floor heating on my manicured feet as I stand up and step into a huge steam shower, taking away my filth in a second. With my warm soft fluffy white towel wrapped around me, I flop back down on my bed big enough for six, and turn to Josh asleep, looking like Jesus wrapped up in a white Egyptian sheet. I'm rich, *rich*! Suddenly £50 notes are like £5 notes. No more frightened of the cost, no more cheap brands, no more hunger. I can now buy food in Waitrose.

I walk around with a wad of cash to buy vodka, cheese, ready meals and plenty of cut-up fruit and veg. Why waste time chopping and dicing when I could be lounging? When browsing I'm often tempted to eat on my rounds for a kick, stealing isn't always about needing, but I don't, because I like this store.

The smiley assistants want to help me pack, they go above and beyond to help me. How do they find these people? Were they the brightest spark from the supermarket with the lower price point down the road? All check-out girls must aspire to work here, they are the chosen few. 'Let me take those bags for you,' they say with a smile. World class they are.

The staff get money off goods, I'd have loved their discount card in a previous life. Wouldn't have made any difference though, seeing as I didn't even have enough money for a penny chew. Could have gone round the back to the food bins I suppose, or do they not dispose of 'best before' food like that in supermarkets any more?

Doughnuts, when I want one, I eat one, bliss. Double chocolate if I so desire, a luxury. 'Look at me, oozing freshly made gunge, soaking into squidgy sponge, lick me.' *Yuck! You remind me of Matthew's hairy arse.* On to the next one, a moist lemon number drizzled with white icing. 'Munch on me.' *But I can't, you remind me of his come in my hair.*

I now have enough money to afford a quality meal, life is good, it doesn't take much for the homeless to be happy. But I'll always be that homeless person, however many meals I eat. I'll always remember that bin, those fishy discarded chips. Homelessness, maybe the staff can see it in me. *Sweet sweet staff, do I look a little shifty?*

I am told to slow down when eating on many an occasion. I can't though, I'm so used to wolfing my food. If I hadn't, some little bastard from the kids' home would have spat in it to own it and scoffed it up himself. But I must remember, I'm not in a kids' home any more, I'm in Waitrose. I must remember, no one is going to take this doughnut from me.

Loaded down with food in Josh's gas guzzler, I was sitting at the traffic lights posing in oversized sunnies when I felt a judder, a vehicle trying to push mine forward. Startled, I glimpsed into my rear-view mirror and saw Uncle Danny's mug grinning right back at me. He poked his yellow beard out of the window of his white van and hollered, 'Hiya! How about a cuddle for your old uncle?'

I rebuffed his big sloppy kisses. Josh was out so I allowed him in.

'Take your dirty stinking boots off!' I screamed as he hovered by the door.

'Jaysus, it's not shite, is it?' he replied, visibly intimidated by my minimalist mansion.

I coaxed him in and he huddled by the hob. 'Now where's the fecking radiator? I'm frozen solid.'

'We've got under-floor heating, you imbecile,' I said scathingly. He glanced at me and, before I could stop him, dropped to the ground like a stone. He lay there spread-eagled, praying the floor would warm him. I couldn't help but find it funny, but didn't dream of letting him know it.

'You simpleton,' I said instead.

'Ahhh, but isn't an uncle who's a simpleton, better than no uncle at all?'

I kicked him. 'Get up will you!' I said and gave him a cuppa.

After he dunked the plainest biscuit I could find into his sugary tea, sucked it to nothing and slurped his weak drink dry, he got up to go, as he couldn't eat anything more than mash and boiled ham and I had neither.

'Even if I did, I wouldn't be offering you any,' I said. *A free meal? I don't think so!*

His teeth had all but rotted away, so he couldn't chew anything. I noticed he squinted now too, his eyes were crying out for glasses. *I could buy them for you, along with a spare pair, but I won't.* I watched him reluctantly leave, calling me 'The Queen of bloody England' on the way out. He was shivering. 'I wish me bones had more flesh, but that shearling jacket would do,' he grumbled, eyeing up Josh's as he walked out the door.

When Josh saw him later, still loitering outside, I told the father of my unborn child that Uncle Danny was a homeless beggar. Not far from the truth.

Uncle Danny, I cannot look at a white van without constantly being reminded of you. I feel like I was in the back of yours so much as a child that I grew up in it. Your van brings back too many memories, so bog off. If you really want a cuddle, you should have been there for me when I was a kid. Back then you had a sofa in your flat, space on your floor, a spare bedroom even. I might have preferred flats with floorboards, but I would have put up with that laminate for the grief you'd have spared me.

How large was I then? Kid-sized, 120 cm high, to be precise. Yes, I'd have grown in body but I'd have kept my needs small, stayed out of your way. Or I could have helped you sell whatever you were shifting that week. 'If the customer is a subject of the Queen, be putting the price up,' you used to say. 'And don't forget to be mean to them, the English like it, it reminds them of their nannies.'

While you attended to your skulduggery, I could have been your look-out. Then you'd never have been caught selling fake perfume in the street. You were seen screaming like a banshee as they manhandled you into the back of a police van. 'The guards are going to crucify me,' you screeched, as your pipe dropped to the floor. 'Arresting me, all because I'm Irish!'

No, they arrested you because what you were doing was illegal.

One time you pulled a sofa from a skip and found a porn mag among its curves. You flicked through and couldn't help but be excited. You sat down to finish yourself off. In I walked. You were mortified, but how we laughed. Probably best we never spoke about that day again.

Where did it all go wrong, Uncle Danny? You're pathetic now, you seem so small to me. You seemed so tall when I was young, I loved you. When you were turfed out of your flat years later, you could have stayed with me. You could now be sharing my food, my home. I'd even have bought you boiled ham. We could have been a family. My fridge would have be your fridge. My kitchen, your kitchen. My wine cellar, though, I'd have had that under lock and key.

Instead you prowl outside my house in your mashed up van, hoping I'll chuck out a trinket so you can sell it in Brick Lane; praying you'll see me, so you can meekly ask me for some money again.

'I'm bollixed, Marni. Just a 20. Pleeeease?'

'Go fuck off across the water you freeloader, I don't want you any more. I am rich now and you are poor. Christ you look it, too. I don't want to be seen dead with you.'

Uncle Danny, it's not my fault that you are poor. Not my fault you were a victim of racism and violence in London in the sixties when notices on the doors of B&Bs said, 'No Blacks, No Irish, No Dogs.' You decided to come here. And later, when people thought all Irish were bombers, you had a gun put to your head, were arrested and accused of being one of the Guildford Four.

For years after, you were stopped by the police. Your van was checked, your licence was checked. 'What about my arse, officer? You forgot to check that!'

'I am persecuted, so I am,' you said to me.

Wow, I didn't know you knew such a long word. So what if the English were against you! You should have made something of yourself, loser. I did.

You know, the suffering you are going through now is only one tenth of what I've been through.

And when you almost freeze to death this winter in the back of your van on a mouldy towel as your mattress, poor, hungry and alone, think of me larging it around my Christmas tree. I will not be thinking of you.

Irish portions

How did Josh not notice this eejit on our doorstep, that my old flat was council and my accent was fake, bar a few correctly pronounced words? That my clothes were mostly cheap, my tits made of silicone and that I never paid for anything? He never met my mother, never even asked after my father. He belonged to a rare breed of man who didn't question who I was. Class was not an issue because he was descended from immigrants, like me. Money was not a worry because compared to me he was rich.

The Electric, 192 and E&O. I knew all the waiters in the classy establishments in the hood, Josh knew the owners. He thought it amusing; I didn't care.

I got a catty comment from a waitress I used to work with, while Josh was on the phone and she was serving me a cheese soufflé.

'Haven't you done well.' *Yes, jealous cow, I have.*

Later, she dropped a drink. I sneered, pretending to love her embarrassment. Truth was, I found it very hard not to get out of my seat to help her mop it up. I was so used to being on the other side.

We left a big tip. I didn't want her putting hairs in my food next time I came. Or gobbing in the mayo. One of my old tricks.

Come Sunday we were back again, this time for the roast. They did the best Yorkshire puddings. My plate had to be piled high. Poor people like large portions, I call them 'Irish' portions.

'It's a sign of love,' I informed Josh, 'The more I give, the more it makes me happy.' He thought it crude.

'Food should be presented in small quantities,' he told me, while a waiter served him a sliver of beef. He would say that, he comes from a different class, his tummy never rumbled. Unless I was cooking. My Sunday roast was rank. Bloodied chicken and charred potatoes served on a plate. As a veggie, I couldn't taste the meat. So we'd go out again.

Having found out about the poor state of my cooking, Josh sent me on a couple of courses at Books for Cooks. *Please! Cooking does nothing for me!* It didn't occur to me that it might do something for him. The women on those courses, where did they come from? Far too privileged for my liking, I couldn't bear sitting next to them so I walked out – shame, the chef was amazing – and shopped in Portobello. I bought a delicious dish from Mr Christian's, ruined it with hot sauce and served it up as my own. It was inedible. Josh gave up.

'I'll cook from now on,' he said, with a sigh.

Mission accomplished!

Someone else's property
June 2002

Mum! Mum! I got married, Mum. A lovely man married me.

We were married at Chelsea register office, with my mother dribbling in her council flat two minutes away. I didn't make Josh marry me. He asked, while I was on the loo. I nearly fell off it in surprise.

'You're not so bad,' he said fondly. 'Anyway, you've trapped me now.'

He couldn't quite say 'I love you', but he did say, 'I love your long toe.' I have a long toe, apparently it's a sign of creativity. That was good enough for me, because I knew he would grow to love all of my toes and the rest of me in time. I couldn't believe my dream had come true, not in the traditional manner, mind, but that didn't matter. I got the most important bit, the diamond, it was in the bank waiting for a wife. Me!

I was so happy not to have a big wedding. All that pomp, Uncle Danny shaming me. A bunch of dysfunctional loser eating all the free cake. God forbid my previous indiscretions should be found out by loose mouths drunk from Cristal champagne. With just two witnesses, it was goodbye to the old me. My name now changed. Relief: I was under the radar.

Matthew, you will find it harder to locate me now. I am someone else's property.

We texted our friends to inform them of our union over afternoon tea in Knightsbridge. Most were miffed we had done them out of a big party, calling us 'tight bastards'. Nice.

True, my dress was only 20 quid from a vintage fashion fair and his suit was one previously worn at a funeral, but it wasn't about the money, it was what *I* wanted. Plus Josh had 300 relatives twice removed that he'd have had to invite, so he was more than content with my decision.

We rolled on to our members' club for a drink. The amount of mates who turned up was overwhelming. Now the free champagne was flowing there were positive vibes all round, apart from one haughty ex-shag of his. 'I must admit I was a bit surprised. I didn't think he'd go for a girl like you, he usually prefers people like me.' That hurt, and on my wedding day! Not being smart always came back to haunt me. She must have despised me, but I ignored her for the moment because I had won the prize, dreams do come true. I didn't let her comment go. When her back was turned, I dribbled in her champagne. Then got annoyed with myself for being a wanker.

Watch out for me, middle-class person, because I am scathing of you. I wish I wasn't, but I don't like you because you have had it easy and I have not. I am now ensconced in your close little circle, but you are so thick-skinned, you don't notice I am not one of you. When you ask me to your ladies' lunch, I play at being your class, I play at being you. Then I ruin it.

Taking out your roasted vegetables from your slate-grey Aga, you delicately arrange them on a ceramic dish with torn buffalo mozzarella. While you prepare our drinks, you kindly ask me to place lunch on your table, decorated with wildflowers picked from your garden.

I feel disconnected. I think to myself, this is not real, so pretentious, what an arse, who does she think she is? If you could hear me you'd answer gently, 'This is my life.

I am just a normal person doing things that are normal to me.'

But it's too late. That glistening on your perfectly roasted parsnips is not extra virgin olive oil lovingly drizzled on, it's my spit, my contribution to this laughable event.

I don't want to do that, but I can't help it. I like you and I hate you at the same time. It's only because I want to be middle class myself. Christ, I married into the middle classes, does that not make me one of you?

Semantics

Shit, shit, shit. I now have to learn to have sex-with-a-husband sex without thinking he's a monster. Apparently it's called making love. It's difficult, like yoga. It makes me raw, it also makes me fart. I have to concentrate so hard to not think of anything bad, but paedophiles keep popping into my head. *Open up now, there's a good girl. Good girl! That's it, much better!*

I can't be bothered to make love, it's too much like hard work. But I must bother, must make the effort, appear to be making love, not be a whore *all* the time. If Josh was a stranger I could switch off, be a robot, do all the right moves, job done. But with someone I love, trust, adore, a husband, my husband, I am vulnerable. It's far too painful, so I act like I'm with a stranger, he's none the wiser, he thinks I am the ultimate wife. When Josh buys me diamonds I instinctively switch into whore mode and give him any orifice he wants, not that he is particularly interested in the other hole. I am consequently laden with jewels.

Most of my relationships have been like this. Haven't I always been prostituting myself? If a man bought me dinner, it was his meal ticket to my mouth. An expensive bag, 'Anything you want, baby!' Matthew had taught me that. It's just a matter of semantics. I guess I will always be 'a prostitute', I'm just my husband's prostitute now. Blow jobs in the kitchen, acrobatics in the bedroom and when it's over, I give him green tea. He feels good; I feel nothing. My past seems to have penetrated everything. There's no escape: Matthew is everywhere.

Our house was just a few streets away from the home. I tried so hard to separate myself from that place. Some days I succeeded. I could stand at the entrance and smell the institutionalised food being cooked for the current wards of court and not plunge into gloom. I had learnt to bury those memories; I had too much to lose. My husband had no idea a children's home even existed round the corner and I wasn't about to tell him either. I was in my new life and loving it.

I behaved like a lottery winner and shopped till I dropped in the now so fashionable Westbourne Grove. I ran from designer store to store and grabbed all I could with the shiny new credit card Josh had given me. Brora cashmere was not to be desired, it was to be worn. Louboutins once a fantasy, now a reality. And the prize: a Chanel handbag.

I was in the big league but irked at how the shop girls treated me. The bitches didn't even offer me champagne till I made a vulgar transaction, then they licked my arse as I passed the latest Pucci and purposely knocked it to the floor. I can easily forget I was once poor.

Security in these swanky stores just wouldn't stop following me around. *Bor-ing*. I was sure the guard thought I was about to steal the Prada bikini I was holding, even though I had my Chanel swinging from my toned arm jangling with diamond bracelets.

Piss off! I am rich, can't you see? No one was duped by the diamonds, it seemed. I sauntered towards the till and pulled out wads of crispy new notes. The snooty shop girl looked me up and down and noticed my figure was adorned with quality clothes. Chloe skinny jeans under a floaty Stella blouse that concealed a neat little bump. Soles covered in a red lacquer. The assistant smelt perfume, not eau de toilette. Admired an expensive blow-dry over a strong bone structure, spoilt by a face that had obviously had work done on it. I fluttered fake eyelashes and broke into an award-winning grin, showing off my bleached white teeth. I finished by saying, 'Thank you,' in a cultivated tone and drifted away. She was steaming with jealousy.

Shop girl, never ever wish to be me. I only have half a life. The other half is in a box I'm too scared to open.

She also didn't trust me. She was canny. She knew I was not what I seemed.

I'm not quite right, I don't know why. A bit like a bloke in a jacket too big. It must be that look of homelessness.

The way I hold myself, the slight stoop from the weight of woe dragging me down. The way my eyes dart round nervously thinking, *Someone's going to get me.* The guilty look that a former petty thief can never quite shake off. Shop girl nods at security.

With my new purchase, I meandered over to lingerie, brushing past the big man in his little uniform, brushing him with my tits. I gave him daggers and disappeared into the changing room with my arms full of designer knickers. He was watching me far too closely. *Fucking wanker!* Smiling to myself, I pulled off my knickers and slid on one of their silk G-strings. Then, with the label sticking uncomfortably into my creases, I scarpered, leaving my soiled ones behind. *That'll teach you, Security, for following me around. After all, it's what you expect from me. And I don't like to disappoint.*

What a kick! My well-brought-up man doesn't know about this rank side of my personality or the life I used to lead, and I will never tell him.

There was no more walking to the post office to pick up Mum's benefit on a Monday morning for me any more. Now it's a quick cappuccino in a place I could never have afforded before. These days I avoid Monday mornings if I need to go to the post office, preferring the more peaceful afternoons. The desperate don't wait till after lunch, they are too bloody hungry.

There was no more carrying a blue bag with a broken zip to the launderette every fortnight, if I was lucky. I used to hate wearing the same knickers for several days in a row. Praying someone had left the dregs of their laundry powder in a cup on the side. Spending hours watching my load. Swinging my feet under the wooden bench with nothing to read but the instructions.

Service must be in 'stand by' mode.
The control knob must be in 'ready' mode.
Press once for quick wash twice for soak.
Hold for Cotton.
Press for Delicates.
Release for Pleats.
No shoes allowed.
No foreign coins.
Supervise your children.

The harsh lighting was giving me a headache. I was hungry. Should my last 20p be on dry laundry or a large packet of crisps? Lugging home damp clothes, I went for the latter. My belly was rumbling in the jungle again and I could not ignore it. Back in the chaotic flat, I stretched out sheets over sofas, pyjamas over chairs, socks on the broken banisters, hoping they'd all dry in time for bed.

When I walk past a launderette now, I quicken my pace, afraid to look at the girl waiting endlessly in there. If we lock eyes, I will become her and I will once again feel the panic of being poor.

No more buses, please. They are miserable, claustrophobic spaces to me.

Look at commuters' faces, wishing they were in my car and not on the bus, crammed in. Jostling for space, stepping on each other's toes. An elbow in the head, a bosom in the back, a thigh pressed inappropriately. The smell of stale breath, mothballs and chip fat. The windows steam up from their body heat.

When a bus stops beside me now, I do not board because all I see is Matthew relieving himself on the back seat. His come soaked into the red checked fabric then on to the arse of the next passenger seated there. At times I didn't even have the bus fare, so I walked.

No more walking for me, it reminds me of being destitute. I can't even bring myself to take my new wellies out for a stroll. It's an official black cab for me now, never any old car where I fucked for the fare.

Will my dream ever end? I am afraid, never drinking more than a measure of Grey Goose in a tumbler with ice. Down in one. I need it. I so want another, but I don't. I will talk, my past will spill out, so I stop myself. Say too much and Josh might get rid of me. Will I ever be able to trust him not to judge me? Control, I must always be in control.

'Your da is asking after ya!' hollered Uncle Danny from the street.

'Like I give a shit,' I shouted back.

Dear Dad,
I have been told that when my mother and I were poor, you were rich. You had shops all over London.

The king of the tourist trade, you were. If it was naff,
you sold it. You had property too and the money came
pouring in. You were living it up, while we were in
our council flat starving. You left me to rot, while
you lived in a penthouse by Kensington Park. Did
you not see me through your window sitting on a
swing? Eating my last-ever piece of fried chicken
wing? Pushing myself higher and higher wishing I
had you? And now you are poor from the crash and
you hear I am rich, you want to see me. What kind of
man are you? A man who was too greedy to give up
one of your rentals to the mother of your own child.
Too tight to give her money, too selfish to notice she
was ill, too heartless to ask after your own daughter.
Vulture, fuck off! Go rot with the rest of the rellies.
Dad, you are dead to me.

A circus
July 2002

Josh got tickets to a children of abuse charity ball. Most
of West London were clamouring to go, so naturally I
felt I had to.

We arrived in a limo for a laugh, photographers fought
for a photo. Deflated that they retreated on the realisation
we were not famous, severely bruising my ego. They ran
to celebs in fairy-tale outfits. Top designer dresses, worth
thousands, worn once. And the jewels! I'd have got rich
by nicking just one earring. Tempting.

The interior was lush, the raffle ridiculous, the auction a madness. Who's going to spend 60 grand to have dinner with some fading famous actress? *Two hundred thousand for a week on my private island! Here, I'll even throw in my watch! Get your portrait taken by the photographer of the moment, only 65 grand! Design your very own diamond ring from one of the greatest jewellery houses ever, a snip at 100,000!*

The worst bit was when they got some poor little victim to speak about her past. Talk about a Victorian freak show. They wheeled her out for the rich to gawp at. She was well groomed now, of course, they chose well, at least she could string a sentence together.

When she started going into detail about the sex acts she had to perform as a child, I had to walk out, too close to home for me. Others left in a hurry too, probably for a wank after being turned on by the poor speaker's intimate description of abuse.

Why do people love to hear the nitty gritty of it all? The more intimate she got, the louder the gasps. The more emotional she got, the louder the moaning, ending in a crescendo of orgasms. The audience, spent, were putty in her hands. Out came their hankies and their big fat chequebooks. They scribbled huge amounts with their Montblanc pens, and handed their cheques in, stained and smudged, to the pretty Sloane brought down from accounts to help out for the evening. They would have normally smacked her pert bottom, but at that moment it seemed inappropriate, at least they knew when to behave.

The speaker had just been fucked by over a thousand people in order to get that cash. She had prostituted herself for a charity that would use most of the money on renting a prestigious West End building in order to maintain its high status. The victim had to relive her nightmare to the rich who in four minutes flat forgot all about her, as a has-been band came on to lighten the mood.

Why don't they just send a cheque in the post instead? 'Look at me, I am so generous, supporting the poor, the abused, the beaten. I am bidding higher than you for a car I don't want, in order to show I have more money than all of you!'

Why don't they just force all the needy to give blow jobs to the rich, I thought the way the victim spoke was only a step away from that. Do away with these balls and send a donation, then the poor speaker won't go home and perhaps self harm, give herself so much physical pain that she forgets.

Megalomania! It's a circus, leaving me with a very bad taste in my mouth.

Proceed with caution
October 2002

Josh said, 'We must get life insurance.' That came out of nowhere.

The life insurance man said, 'You must have an HIV test.'

Jesus, I'd never thought of that. What if I have HIV and give it to my unborn child? Christ, I might have given it to half of West London.

I was nervous, my husband was nervous. He'd been a slapper too, putting it about like there was no tomorrow. I was forever bumping into ex-shags of his and non-shags who wished they had been. One woman came up to me at a party after staring at me all night and said, 'Hi, I am the only girl in West Eleven your husband hasn't slept with.'

How am I supposed to respond to that? Think!

'I can see why, dear,' I said, coolly.

We went to our private doctor in Portobello and sat in his plush office. 'The samples will be sent off, you will receive a letter in a few days.'

A few days? How are we supposed to coast that? Our lives could change forever.

We both agreed that we didn't really want to read a letter like that on our own, so we waited and opened them together.

'You first.'

'No, you first.'

'Together. One, two, three – open.'

Both negative – what relief! People say it's good to do activities with your family. A family that opens letters together, stays together. If I had opened that rent arrears letter of my mother's, I might not have been evicted, gone into a home, been groomed, raped, prostituted myself, ending up in fear of an HIV test.

*

I could now feel the kicks of my baby. I might not shag for money any more but I was soon to be a mother and I was still a carer. I must not forget that. My being a carer to my mother was not a desirable subject matter to my fair-weather friends. If I talked clothes, houses, interiors, furniture, food, they gravitated towards me, but at the mere mention of schizophrenia they retreated. I couldn't talk to anyone about this hidden job I had; making sure she was fed, not dead and lying in dirty sheets. My secret career was lonely.

When I actually met someone from the mental health sector, I told them with a rush of words about my mother. We spoke another language about the pros and cons of section 3, section 28, and the side effects of mood stabilisers. What an interesting conversation to me, dull as fuck to most, but how great to chat to someone if only for a few minutes who had an insight into my other life.

I saw my mum whenever I could and on the days that I didn't, it bothered me. It took courage to see her, my heart always heavy when we said goodbye. I had been campaigning for years to get her out of her hard-to-let, dingy flat. Letters back and forth to the council. Meetings, hearings, tribunals. Her flat may have been grotty but it did have two bedrooms. I thought there was supposed to be a shortage.

But at last came a letter from the council that I was not afraid to open. My mum had been offered a flat in the poshest part of Chelsea. In the very street we'd been evicted from, all those years ago. Back then, they had used the excuse of unpaid rent to get rid of us. When they'd got their hands on it, they'd done a refurb to house old people; now she was old, she fitted their remit. After nearly 20 years in the gutter, on the street, in a B&B, a squat, a lock-up, a hospital, a hard-to-let flat, she was back.

I had hounded the council until I'd got what I wanted for my mother, now perhaps it was time to hound them to get what I wanted for me: lots of money for placing me with a predatory paedophile.

> Dear Council,
>   You got a neglected girl ready to be fucked by a perv. It's not too late to sue. Shall I or shan't I? I'll pick the petals from a daisy and decide. The reputation of my old borough relies on whether it's a yes or a no. There's no time limit for a heinous crime.

I walked with pleasure through leafy streets to less leafy streets to tell my mother the good news.

'Hello, hello, no mop today. And where's Tesco? Stuffed full of rubbish, I see.'

I couldn't get to her door as an overstuffed chair now jammed the entrance.

'Blue door, I am sorry, this time I'm determined to go through you, whether my mother likes it or not.'

I climbed over the chair with difficulty. My bump was beginning to get in the way. I pulled wooden strips from the rotting windowpane, carefully removed the glass, crawled through and retched at the smell of shit and cheap soap.

Inside, clothes were stuffed in bin liners, a moth-eaten cardigan tumbled out of a box. Shoes were piled high, none matching. The bath was filled with shampoo bottles, three plastic bowls and four showerheads, three of them broken. There were mouldy towels on the floor, a blocked loo full of sodden loo rolls and shit. The kitchen had dirty dishes on every surface, together with cans of paint and out of date food. Bloated sausages, black bananas, rotting apples and rank milk bursting from its carton. Peas were squashed into the cracked tiled floor. Her flat was a tip. *Where are you, Mum?*

I smelt her out. I stepped over rubbish and pushed aside fabric, finding her in a bed drenched in sweat. She was incoherent, desperately I tried to get through. So into herself she did not see me, but God saw her, he shone a slither of sun on her face and said:

All is not lost, your child is with child; there's hope.
Find peace, find courage, find Me; you will have life
again.

I forged her signature on the acceptance letter for the new flat and chucked out every last scrap of her rubbish while my belly bounced to her verbal abuse. The baby didn't like the tone of her voice, neither did I.

'I am going to kill you *and* that thing!' she roared, stabbing at my bump with her gnarled forefinger. 'Thing!

What is that *thing*?' I jumped back and protected my baby with my hand. This was not how I'd imagined their first encounter.

Hostile cows

I see people, mobiles in pockets, earphones connected. Phones ring, a conversation. Hands gesturing, mouths moving, heads shaking, holding nothing, looking mad; there are many reminding me of my mother.

I rang the mental health unit and got her locked up under section 3 for six months this time. By the time they turned up she was trying to scrape the white stucco off the front of her new building with a trowel. She was extremely aggressive when asked to stop.

'GRRR, FUCK FUCK FUCK OFF!'

'Rabid dog' was the whispered description. The doctors took her away in a police van again, so undignified. I was surprised at my lack of emotion this time. I was still seething from her going near my bump. I loved this baby, even though I had fought those feelings, just in case it died.

The mental health ward was mixed, as usual. Great big men, gaunt men, pathetic men and distinguished looking men, all in standard-issue dressing gowns. Beside them, women of every shape and size, cowering by the nurses' station, most of them with dodgy haircuts they'd done themselves. At that moment, I wished my mum had been stillborn: she'd not be dead in the head like them.

I am not frightened of mad people; I understand their behaviour. If you come across hostile cows, the solution is not to provoke; they may follow you, trample you to death. They wouldn't have meant it, they couldn't help it, they are simply out of control. When it comes to mad people the ignorant are afraid. Tabloids don't help, scaring the public with stories of 'paranoid schizophrenics', murdering madmen. Very rare, they are more likely to murder themselves.

The ward was calm, not the slightest bit threatening, because the patients had been held down and given the 'zombie' injection. They were shuffling around in slow motion with silly grins and zoned-out stares. Was it me who had the problem? *Am I walking too fast? Talking too fast? Am I in the loony bin and my mum is visiting me?*

Her room was tiny with no door, just one of a series of cubicles off a long corridor. The decor, uneventful. Why can't they have nice furniture? I am sure these patients would appreciate a good aesthetic, my mother certainly would. We're all affected by our surroundings, even the mad. My mum may be zoned out, but I'm sure she still minds that austere metal bed with the thin brown bedspread, those flimsy orange curtains that let in the light, those high-backed institutional chairs with piss stains on them, that harsh lighting you only find in institutions and launderettes, no good for the complexion. And the smell, I am sure the mad very much mind that smell. What is it? Disinfectant? Sweat? Urine? Lunch? Smells of forgotten people to me.

My mother was one of those zombies again, sitting there, staring, in an institutional chair. Her body covering the last patient's mess. Slowly she turned to me and asked, 'Can I borrow your electric piano to play to the other patients?' I didn't know she could play. She couldn't.

I said, 'Yes, of course.' I handed it in to the nurses' desk the next day. I did not go up to see her. Too painful. *Can you feel my sadness, Mum? It's killing me.*

My husband saw me crying. It frightened him, I never cry.

'What's wrong?' he asked, alarmed.

'Hormones,' I replied.

Please don't make me talk about it. My heart hurts so much when I speak of my mother. Don't make me answer questions, I will only tell you lies. The truth feels so tight in my chest, so tight I cannot breathe.

'Just get me some cheese!'

Cheese sandwiches
December 2002

Bloody hell, how am I supposed to have sex with a great big bump that's kicking me every five minutes? Lucky I am well versed in blow jobs. With a lick of my lips, job done.

Contractions, my husband was shell-shocked when my body took over. He ordered a cab and got £400 from the cashpoint.

'Why did you do that?' I asked, as we raced into town.

'I didn't know what else to do.'

I gave birth to my baby in a bath in the most expensive hospital in the land with no drugs and no complications. Waste of money. If I'd have known she was going to shoot out like that, I'd have had her at home.

I look down at my daughter made of cheese sandwiches. I am in love with this sweet little thing. I had been blessed. Why me? I am so lucky. The pain of love, I am not so dead after all. *My darling girl, you have brought me back to life.*

But my baby is a *girl*! This scares me. How am I supposed to protect a *girl*? Things happened to me, I must not let things happen to her. She has to have a normal, happy life. *Fuck, fuck, fuck.* The paranoia of paedophilia has really begun. *I am out of control.*

Holding her tight in my arms, I whisper to her, 'I'll be the best mum ever, protect you from all the evils, give you everything in life I did not have.' *So 'council' of me to say that.* 'And when you're older,' I continue, 'I promise I will let you choose your own religion, your own clothes, your own food. Bacon, egg and sausage will be served till you decline; I'll not push being a vegetarian on anyone. And church will never be frequented unless you ask.'

I will fight with God, fight to keep my daughter thriving. *God, bring it on, let the battle begin. She is mine and You will not take her from me!*

My mum was escorted to my suite to meet my brand new bundle. She got a few odd looks from the nurses, but they were too polite to comment on her involuntary movements of the mouth and how it took her two years to float down the hospital hall to greet me, flanked by a psychiatric minder from her current abode.

When she laid eyes on her granddaughter, and my husband laid eyes on my mother, and I laid eyes on both, it was emotional. My mum had lost weight, aged four decades, and, even though she was drugged up, I could tell there was a new lucidity there. She had even plaited her ridiculously long hair. At the same time I gave birth to my baby, she had been reborn.

God, if You exist, which You know I doubt, thank You for giving me back my mum. Hope Josh is not too freaked out by having a care in the community patient as his mother-in-law.

What a very happy Christmas.

I kept my daughter's placenta. I have it in the freezer. Wherever I go, it goes, that placenta is a part of me. It's fun taking it out of the freezer at dinner parties. Friends are fascinated by its size, nearly the same as a newborn. They are not too keen on the smell though, like a dead person. I refuse to fry it up with onions and eat it like some friend suggested. Anyway I can't, I'm a vegetarian.

As a vegetarian, if I ate myself, would I be considered not to be a vegetarian any more? Would eating my own placenta count as meat? Technically, it's not my placenta, it's my daughter's, so I am not actually eating myself. But I am because I created it. Is that cannibalism then?

I could do other things apart from eating it. Bury it and plant a tree on top, for example. But I like having it around. I have decided to give it to my daughter on her 18th.

I can't get used to going home to a husband with a child by my side. *Is this what a normal life is?* I wake up and remember that I am not dreaming. There's a deep happiness in my chest. It's not money that's making me feel good, it's family. I now have my very own family. I will hold on to this joy so that when my mood next dips, racing down fast, this will lift me out of my bottomless pit.

I have too many staff. A maternity nurse for the moment with a nanny coming in March. The bitch of a nurse gets moody if I hold *my* baby. What am *I* supposed to do apart from get bored? Dangerous, I might give in to temptation and have a line as long as my arm. So I relegate her to the night shift. Maybe I should just get rid of her and do it myself, my mum did. Second thoughts, it's quite nice to have a rest when I want. Maybe I'll luxuriate in all this for just a little bit longer.

No, I don't like it. I want to be with my baby. So I get rid of the maternity nurse early with full pay, and inform the nanny she's not coming.

'I apologise. I made these stupid plans before I saw my baby.' *Anyway, how do I know you're not a paedophile? I'm sorry but my brain thinks of nothing else. Everyone is a monster to me.*

Voice command
January 2003

Why do we get porn star boobs at the most inappropriate time? My milk has come gushing in, my tits are obscene. I have a screaming baby and a husband who is as hard as a rock, wanting to shove his dick in between my tits until there is no telling what is dripping from them, seeing as milk and come are almost the same colour. My cunt has been stretched to fuck, is rip raw sore, and I've no time to do my pelvic floor exercises. I wish I'd had a caesarean. No, I don't. Well, maybe a little bit.

Go away! I've got dog flaps for a fanny and am so not in the mood.

But Josh is like a dog on heat at the sight of my milky hard tits. So robot whore clicks in and down I go, putting hubby's needs before my own. His dick pumping my mouth while his hands are kneading my tits, pinching my bleeding nipples.

'That fucking *hurts*!' I scream. Not in pleasure like the old days.

Later that day he is staring at me. Dick rising, he is waiting, I oblige yet again. I allow him to touch my raging raw nipples and then move me and the baby to the spare room saying, 'It's because I want you to get a good night's sleep.' *Big fat lie.*

Why can't I tell him to 'Fuck off out of it!' like any other new mum? Because I'm programmed to respond to sexual demands. However tired or ill I am, I'll always say yes.

Bag an abused women, she may be slightly vacant but she'll be cracking in the sack. Like those toys that lie dormant but come to life on voice command, doing tricks at the flick of a switch. Maybe that's how I really got Josh, not because I was pregnant or gave him a blow job every day, it was because he realised he had a shag for life. He saw how I became a live sex show whenever he asked for it, when what I really wanted was just a hug, or a kiss maybe – but I could never tell him that.

For a girl who gets by on how she tarts herself up, being pregnant had been tough. Skinny jeans and knee-high boots were not so hot on a woman in her third trimester. I had noticed my husband had stuck it in me less and I could see why. I'd got fat and stayed in, refusing to go out until the baby was born and I could then do one of those drastic diets. So what if it was bad for me. 'I've got to get back to looking good,' I told myself. My looks were far more important than my health.

'If you want to lose weight, don't eat,' an anorexic friend said to me. So when my girl was born, I had porridge with water and miso soup. My husband wanted a nice bird on his arm not a whale.

I was wrong, he liked me with a bit of weight on. The way my tits shimmied as I walked through the door. The swish sound of my stay-ups, as my thighs rubbed together from too much cheese. I wanted to wear tights really, but he didn't find them sexy. There was a lot of love for me in the bedroom, my man was wild for the new me.

Men don't want us skinny, it's a myth, I thought as he pulled at my flesh. Shame he found me so horny, I just wanted to sleep.

I wish I wasn't quite so shallow, but I have to make myself look good and be desired by my man all the time. I preen myself to an inch of my life, never a hair out of place. I learnt from a young age to always be ready for my next fuck. I am stuck on standby mode, hating it really, until I notice someone else's husband hankering for a feel of me, then I like it. I need to be wanted.

I found out I had an incipient form of cancer. Ironic it was in my fanny, must have been from all those men poisoning me. Lucky I found it. I bled during sex but I had just given birth. I thought it was normal, but my instincts told me to see a doctor.

Zapping those bad cells quickly the gynaecologist told me to be on standby for more. *God, it's not my fault I've been a skank, please don't blame me. Give Matthew the cancer, not me.*

But the word 'cancer' saved me. I didn't want to kill myself any more. No, that's wrong: it was my daughter, she saved me. Giving birth saved me from suicidal thoughts.

Marrying well

I was an inspiration to the beauticians at my local salon. Not because of the cancer scare, but because they felt one of their own had married well. While they busily waxed my vag, they asked me for some pointers. I showed them my tit scars and had fun with the answers.

If you want to marry a rich man, remember:

- Don't ever take someone's reservation in a restaurant, cocktails on someone's tab, a Gucci coat upon leaving, or get into someone else's booked cab. Not in front of him anyway. You are supposed to be a lady, refined.
- Poor equals shit clothes. Shit clothes equals not getting into fancy places where the rich hang out, which means not bagging yourself a rich husband. If you can only afford one thing, make it a good-quality coat. It can be second hand, but get it dry-cleaned. The power of a well-tailored coat! It will make a huge difference, just make sure it doesn't stink.
- Eat. Bones are not sexy to a man unless he is a paedophile.
- Voice. Cockney? Don't speak unless you can fake posh. Having my well-spoken voice, however hard I had to work at it, was the single most important factor in crossing classes.
- Blow jobs. Practise with your mate's willing older brother. There is no man in the world who does not want your pretty mouth round his dick.

- Legs. Never have unwaxed legs, and I shouldn't have to tell you about your fanny. It should be plucked to within an inch of its life. Never shave. No man wants to come up from eating your mound chafed and looking like he's just kissed a man.

- Shoes. You must have well-made shoes. Who needs Prada when there's L.K. Bennett? I was so proud when I saved up and bought my first ever pair. I wore them to death. Those stuck-up bitches on the doors of nightclubs will eyeball you up and down. Look confident and aloof. Let them take in your silky-soft coat, but remember: they must envy your fuck-off shoes.

- Teeth. You can always tell a poor person by the colour of their teeth. Perfectly blow-dried hair? Tick. Well-cut coat? Tick. Expensive shoes? Tick. Yellow teeth? Oh dear. Stained teeth equals poor. Piss poor. Don't give the game away, you've come so far. Don't mess it up when you're so close to winning the big prize. Get your teeth whitened now.

- Accessories. Save up for a classic silk scarf, preferably Hermès. Rich men know their labels. You'll need a black cocktail dress, a good hair cut, but not too short, refined men as a rule like long flowing hair. Finally, you must have a designer handbag. It can be a fake. Then your potential man will have no idea you are poor.

- Network. Save up and become a member of any private club you can. That's how I met my man.

- Tits. If your gran dies and leaves you a couple of thousand, get a tit job. Second thoughts, don't, I regret it. Get those gel things to fill your bra with, and never a grey washed-out bra, please. Just make sure you take the fillets out before petting. Don't let your new man get there first, it will be a huge shock for him and a disaster for you when he walks.
- If you are a little bit clever at all, study – anything. To be on some kind of course is always impressive.
- Save up and travel outside the safe zone. The Costa del Sol will wait for you. Exotic places are fascinating to the rich.
- Do something for charity. Make it for the mad while you're at it.
- Don't be a vegetarian, too awkward when he takes you to his favourite restaurant to share suckling pig.
- Last thing. Let him fall madly in love with you, so in love with you that he can't see life without you, before you meet his parents. They'll see right through you.

Rooftops of Chelsea
October 2003

My mum does not have long to live. Her medication strong; her heart weak, it may stop at any time. Better to have a short not-that-bad-at-the-end-of-it life than a long crap one. So I don't take a single day with her for granted, giving her a cashmere coat as a Christmas prezzy early. 'Wear it now!' *You might be dead by then.*

Lunch and a stroll in a private garden square with her, my baby and the Bugaboo. I now have a key, even though I'm not at all comfortable with its exclusivity.

A scruffy kid peers in. I sense longing and see myself.

Do I dare let you in? Every other mother here is oblivious to your needs, they did not have our life. One more child, they won't notice. Sadly they will. Your lack of cashmere and welly boots will give you away. Your hardness for such a young age, your accent. Don't say a word, not one word. Here, wear my child's cardy and play quietly. Enjoy this rare moment of a club you and I will never belong to.

My mother's psychiatric minder told me that after months in the lock-up, my mum realised she was ill and that she needed medication to keep her stable. She had at last gained insight. I prayed that would help her never to get psychotic again. The day she stops taking those pills is the day she won't be able to see her grandchild any more.

She is of fragile mind, I have to protect her, she can't ever know what happened to me. She's quite stable now, topped up daily on Risperdal. She's come back to life, a bit. I'm beginning to see glimpses of her true personality. I never knew she had a sense of humour, giggling when I mimicked Uncle Danny's voice. I never knew she was so creative, attempting pottery at rehabilitation classes. I never knew she liked to dance. I thought her swirling to Paul Simon was part of the illness. She's a calm and lovely skinny mass moving in slow motion. So regal with her nose in the air, so stylish in her vintage finds; but her hands make me melancholy, so small and wrinkly now, and in the shape of a claw.

Mum, we'll make up for lost time, do all the things my friends did with their mothers all those years ago. We'll do something as simple as shopping for clothes together. Of course, I missed out on you buying me my first bra, my friend took me and told me the facts of life at the same time, which I knew full well already. But there's no point in us thinking about all that now. I have a child, you have a grandchild, we have each other, let's start again. *But no granny babysitting, just in case.*

I take her to Harrods and The Savoy, places she would have been turfed out of a year ago, places *I* would have been turfed out of a year ago. I had almost written her off, now here I am taking her to the top floor of Peter Jones, my favourite place of all.

We look out over the rooftops of Chelsea, with her drinking a cup of Earl Grey, me with my English breakfast tea, the closest thing to builder's I can get here. I chat to her. She only speaks to answer a question, to enquire the time, to request to leave. She can't do much with her life, I am her life. So I give her little things to do, to give her a purpose. Buy booties from Bonpoint, a ring from Cartier, a refund from Harvey Nichols, that type of thing.

I choose not to notice my mother isn't normal until I see other others on the fifth floor fussing. They seem to have an opinion on anything their daughters do. How annoying that must be. *Bet it's great really*. I don't allow myself to look too long, I'll feel empty.

I casually tell her about my wedding. Surprisingly unconcerned with her lack of invitation, she tells me slowly, 'I did the same thing.' She ran off with my dad to a register office in the same borough in the sixties with the obligatory two witnesses.

How it hurts not to have known that till now. Children usually grow up with that kind of knowledge. Not just from stories, from photos in frames on old-fashioned sideboards: 'Who's that fat person with the silly hat in the picture, Mummy?' My mum and dad's marriage only lasted a few years, I will make sure mine lasts a lifetime.

Seeing as my father was mentioned, I gingerly ask more, shit scared that she might flip and smash the cup she's sipping from and shove it in my face. But then I remember she won't, because her emotion is controlled by her medication.

'He came to see you, more than you remember,' she tells me.

My mother begins to scratch her cheek, hard, until red marks appear. I'm too nervous to continue. I change the subject, to distract her from her limited feelings. I don't want her to end up dead before her time. I am on edge, antennae always up for the next negative episode.

Mini me
March 2004

I felt so alive, a type of glow, I had to be pregnant. At eight weeks I had a viability scan. I heard a heartbeat, saw a blob on the scanning machine. A new baby, a sibling for my daughter.

At 12 weeks I had the routine scan. With warmed jelly on my tummy, I tilted my head to see the baby on the screen.

The obstetrician turned it away from me, *Don't turn it away, I want it this time*. I strained to look. 'It's still the same size,' I said, 'it hasn't grown.' Silence. It sank in. How thick was I to not realise what that image meant.

The obstetrician looked at me with sadness and softly said, 'I'm very sorry, but you have lost your baby.'

What was he talking about? I saw the heartbeat, it was alive. I was stunned. Was I in a dream? I laughed, where were my tears? Laughing, laughing, laughing, that displaced emotion thing again.

I spent most of my life hating the idea of being pregnant, but now with one child I desperately wanted two. I wanted children close in age so they could play together, look out for each other when they were eventually orphaned. This was God's doing, He was making me suffer the way my aborted child had suffered, in terrible pain.

I could wait and carry that dead baby in me for six months or more until my body was ready to have a natural miscarriage. Or I could have an operation the next day, to remove the baby and get on with my life. I had carried it for 12 weeks, it had been dead in me for four, I didn't think I could take any more.

All that talk, hope, excitement, gone. I walked from Harley Street to Marylebone in a daze, looking in the Conran Shop for no reason other than diversion. *These shoppers, they have no idea what has happened. Why does life not stop? Why don't people turn to me and acknowledge the death of my baby? Give me five minutes of peace and say, 'I am sorry for your loss'. How dare life carry on as normal.*

My daughter looked at me, her big blue eyes burrowed into my broken soul. She was a toddler, but it was as if she understood completely.

I begged the obstetrician: 'When you scrape the baby out, I don't want to know if was a boy or a girl. It will feel too real, then I'll have to mourn.'

He took a sample of the 'tissue' and found it had a rare chromosomal abnormality, only to be found in girls.

I felt sick and screamed, 'My baby is dead!' That centimetre of tissue was all baby to me. Once a Catholic always a Catholic. I may have been lapsed and angry, but I still held on to its values.

Dear Dead Baby Girl,

Sorry, I don't know what else to call you. Would you like me to give you a name? Mini-me? Mini-Marni? Mini-you.

I wanted you with what I imagine, straight blonde hair and a crooked smile, now ashes in an incinerator. Will I ever have another girl whom I can hug, reassure, guide through puberty, make her proud of her body? Speak to me of periods, boys and sexual relations? Maybe it was God's way of protecting you. If you're not born, you can never be abused.

How can I even attempt to think God is real on days like these? I spiral down into doom. I try and comfort eat, shoving half a bar of chocolate down my throat. But I cannot face the rest, it reminds me of Matthew.

A part of me is dead. Dead so I can look at my underwear disappearing in the washing machine without thinking of Matthew's mess. Dead so I can have sex with Josh without hitting him and screaming at him to, 'Get off me!' It's probably a good thing, otherwise I'd be like my mother, hitting myself with a rolling pin, trying to knock out bad thoughts. But I am not dead, am I? Because the dead have no memory and I can still feel Matthew's hands on me.

I'm itchy, so itchy. In a bath of cold water I scrub my body until my skin is red raw, ridding me of the filth ingrained in my soul.

'Come out! Come out!' But it will never come out, for I wear a cilice, a hair shirt worn as a sign of repentance. I have done wrong.

No, I haven't, a paedophile is to blame.

God help me, is Matthew still out there? He must be free from jail by now. The last time we spoke he said, 'I will find you, wherever you are, even when you're old.'

I feel him waiting. *I am coming to get you. To cut your head off with an axe.*

My boy
July 2005

God smiled on me. Just over a year later I had a son. He too was made from cheese sandwiches, toasted this time. So glad he was not a girl, less chance of being raped. Nor will he be a paedophile. I will teach him to love and respect women from the start. He will not be warped, he will have a normal, happy life.

> *Dear Dad,*
>   *Forgive me for not being a boy. I gave birth to a boy, will that do? And now that you have a grandson, will you come back? I want you to come and meet him. Can you hear me? Maybe you're dead. You used to be dead to me.*

Squatting in the birthing pool, my boy and other matter popped to the surface. I dropped back and lay him on me, while my husband sieved out poo with a colander. With the umbilical cord still attached, we bonded for ten minutes or more before he was whisked off to have a scan.

'He seems to have an indentation in the base of his spine,' the doctor told us. His notes said 'Spina bifida'. *No, no, please, no!*

'Just a deep dimple,' the radiographer explained. *Thank fucking Christ!*

All I could see were pound signs in my husband's eyes, not tears, after our son got the all-clear. 'Right, let's get him home,' he said, 'every hour is costing me in here.'

'No way, I'm staying the night,' I replied as I held my boy.

I heard a huge sigh through the popping of pink champagne. I smiled and languished in my luxurious bed.

FOUR

'The rest of the people will hear of this and be afraid, and never again will such an evil thing be done among you.'

DEUTERONOMY 19:20

The country
July 2007

Matthew put-putted off on his pathetic scooter, when I saw him for the fifth day running. In Portobello market. In a yellow cagoule. *I think it was you anyway.*

On the sixth day of seeing him, I decided I would be the one who went away.

I said to Josh, 'I want our children to wake up every morning and breathe in fresh country air.'

It has got absolutely nothing to do with a paedophile in a cagoule following me.

I was more than ready to go. I also couldn't bear bumping into Uncle Danny who'd then forever be begging me for ten quid.

If I want my children to have a normal life, I need to get them away from my past. It felt like it wouldn't be long before Matthew killed me, then entered my 'nice, warm, twitching body'.

I fucked off. I didn't even wait for the house to be sold. We moved to a Georgian pile in the country with Cadogan Tate and those fit boys in tow.

Losing everything when I was a child has turned me into a hard-line minimalist. Nothing holds sentimental value for me. If I don't use something for a while, be it a chair or a chopping board, I throw it out. If my children don't play with a toy for a few months, it goes to the charity shop. I must be the only person with a clear attic. Why would I want to keep stuff? For the joy of old times? The past is too painful. I can walk away from all of it.

I don't care whether I live in a house for six months or five years. When I leave, I don't look back. A house is only bricks and mortar to me, what makes a house a home is a family. I have no anchor, I'm free to roam as long as they move with me. My family will want to settle one day, make roots, so my next attempt will be in the country. I'm going on an 'adventure'.

The posh county

I can't shit without everyone knowing in this county. It's stifling. I have to be careful because I cannot untell my story. If they hear it, these country folk will see me as flawed, a person not to be trusted.

But I've been judged all my life, I've had enough. If people are going to dislike me, let it be for my lack of riding skills, not for my threesome when unwittingly pregnant. Only the impartial could ever be my friend.

I stick my hand out and say 'Hello' politely to everyone I see, just like an American. I could make up a new identity,

I could make up anything, but I don't. I've been lying all my life, so I say nothing. The new people I meet think I'm here because I want to give my children an Enid Blyton *Famous Five* kind of life. Let them think what they like. I won't even mind if they think I'm boring, it's better than them thinking I'm a cunt. I wish I could stop being a vegetarian though, I am bound to be seen as kooky.

I notice the smell of manure on the fields. I breathe in. I like it. Incessant mooing, I cannot sleep. Why are the cows making that dreadful noise? Moo-ooo-OOO! Because their children have been taken away for beef. Endless screaming till they forget. Then they remember and the mooing starts again. Moo-ooo-OOO! Moo-ooo-OOO! Moo-ooo-OOO! The sound of grieving from a mother whose child is now Sunday roast.

Gastropubs, farmers, footpaths, dogs free of leads, black Labradors, polite hellos and road kill the size of children.

I have arrived into a world where it seems no woman works, of ladies' lunches and tennis socials, the posh county. Where girls in pearls and Brora retire to when they get married. Acutely aware my voice is my passport, I dare not drop a T. I'm back with my childhood neighbour, with her neat little Alice band, all over again. I have to fit in! *I may not be your tribe, but can I still belong? I now have a Land Rover, will that do?*

We are the new 'sharks' from London. I'm not happy with that description, but the country lot see us as so.

At least we weren't weekenders, they are not welcome around these parts. And the questions begin. 'Where are you from?'

Please, don't ask me about my parents. I'll be defensive, clam up, give you one-word answers. My life was not the same as yours, talking about it makes me very chippy.

I may have moved to the country but, weather permitting, my designer high heels have not left my feet, handy because my husband and I have been invited to every dinner going. I'm really not a good dinner guest, though. I make people feel awkward from my lack of understanding social norms. I can't decipher which stories in my life are appropriate. I haven't any throwaway anecdotes to tell about my childhood, apart from, 'I pissed on a swing and hoped no one would notice.' I'm so desensitised by the heavy stuff, I usually drop bomb after bomb into light-hearted conversations, so I sit tight and let Josh do the talking.

They want to find out how much money we've got, among other things. Terribly vulgar. These dinners should be fun, but they feel like job interviews.

'Sit soft! First-time buyers?' jokes the toffy host wearing a Boden woolly jumper.

'No,' Josh replies. That is the truth. My husband went to a fee-paying school and so did I, even though my stay there was only for a minute.

'Family money or new money?' he quips. 'From prostitution or drugs?' he guffaws.

Careful what you say in jest, for it may be the truth.

To amuse him I reply, 'It's uncouth to talk about such things. Don't you know?'

You can't get a soya latte in the country, but the white stuff is everywhere. There's no shortage of illegal substances out here. I'm trying so hard to stay off them, but I know where to go if I fall.

> *Dear Country Lot,*
> *Please, please don't offer me drugs. I'm a caner.*
> *My behaviour will get ugly. I can't stop at one line.*
> *I'll do ten and want to hurt someone, and almost*
> *certainly a man. Rape him with his car keys, lick him*
> *where he bleeds.*

These ladies are effortless at making dinner, even the ones without a domestic, and these gentlemen are very well-to-do. Seems like everyone in this lush county is related to the Queen or served her country. In London I didn't know a single soldier, let alone an officer. Now I'm sitting next to a brigadier for Bellinis and a general at dinner. They all seem very genial. I wonder what they think about me? Don't let them find out my lineage, they'll kill me. Maybe I'll tell them I'm Irish in time, I'd better wait until they like me first. Probably the only Irish they know are the ones they shot, half of them being my relatives, no doubt. They have to save their Sovereign. I'm a second-class citizen.

This is surreal. How did I get here? Why didn't I know, when I was in care, that one day I'd end up hanging out with these high rankers? It would have offered me some respite in my despair.

Once I get used to the plums in their mouths and their stripy shirts, I surprise myself by liking them. So civil, such manners, and they seem to have an old-fashioned sense of family. They make me ashamed of my lack of finesse. *I am trying so hard but it's difficult. Living with my mum, rudeness was the norm, picked up by osmosis. I'm terribly sorry.*

Everyone does 'Thank you for supper' letters in the country, on personally printed notepaper. A 'thank you' by text is not enough, how tiresome. I buy a Montblanc and order up notelets from Smythson. Gosh, all these gushing letters I have to pen, so time-consuming. Plus my writing is like a six-year-old's and I simply don't know what to say.

'Thank you for my meal, it was very nice,' needs to turn into a two page poetic scrawl of how it was, 'Fantastic! Lady Bla Bla was simply delightful, the dauphinoise delicious, I simply adore cream, a pleasant surprise as I am usually served shit.' I beg my husband to do it, he knows the form. Reluctantly, he agrees.

I'm worried, I don't think I can keep up appearances for much longer.

My kids' school is amazing. Endless acres for them to play in, all kinds of activities to enjoy, and sport every single day. It would be difficult to put them back into a postage stamp sized playground in London after this place. My old school was a joke compared to this.

But what of this privilege? My kids now think everyone owns a swimming pool, a tennis court and a castle Up North. I've got to keep them grounded. This county isn't exactly multi-cultural either. Frequent trips to London are needed for my children to be well-rounded individuals. I'll take them to see a few relatives in their high rises while I'm at it, that should to do the trick.

I collect my children from the playground, wave and smile at the other mums, walk over and join in on their chit-chat. I'm just like them, gossiping away, then I remember I'm nothing like them at all. My manner is studied, I have to watch what I say, I'm naturally inappropriate. I'm also not posh. I think I have more in common with the teachers than the parents – actually, the teachers are posher than me. The dinner ladies then. No, I can see that they too are from far better families than mine. The cleaners? No, turns out they're from solid stock as well. Anyone? No, I have nothing in common with anyone. I'm an imposter. The teachers have an inkling. I swear all the fucking time.

Wait, there are bursary kids here. When I look at them, I see me, they are the ones I have something in common with. No, they are from nice normal families and are happy. I never was.

*

In idle moments, I wonder what Matthew is doing right now. I have to find out. Is he still on the sex offenders' list? He could be back working with children. Just because he's old doesn't mean he can't destroy. He'll still have long fingers and a wrinkly snake. I need to find him.

So I hire a private detective to discover his exact whereabouts. There could be good news, he might be dead already. If he is, I won't believe it. 'I'm going to pretend I've died,' he told me once, 'so I can get hold of my life insurance.' *But how could you? You'd be dead!*

So far the detective has only found who Matthew married. Pathetic, I could have told him that. I get rid of him and search for a big boy to play with, someone in Intelligence maybe. I sit next to one at dinner. Everyone knows but pretends not to. 'Well, is he?' I whisper fascinated.

'Shhh! That information is on a need-to-know basis.'

Jesus, don't tell me they think I'm a security risk. I feel like I'm back in my old school playground.

I decide to adopt a country pursuit, riding. Never again. Useless, I shall stick with what I know. A scrambler. Matthew bought me one when I was young. But I kept braking too hard, shooting over the handlebars and I couldn't afford to fix it. I lay still where I fell, in the shape of a rag doll, remembering my time through the air. That was the moment I decided to do a parachute jump. I threw myself from a wing at dusk and pissed myself as I tumbled down head first, I had forgotten the drill. Matthew upgraded me to a car, but the brakes had been fiddled with and failed at 40. On purpose? I wrote it off. He gave me so many nice things for fucking him.

Country folk, if you end up finding out about me, instead of calling me a skank, call me a victim. No, a survivor. A winner not a loser. I'll feel less shame.

No one can see my past and with my fake airs and graces, I could almost be one of the mothers. But I'm getting restless, nobody wants to come to mine any more, I have a reputation for serving vodka and not much else. I just clam up when it comes to cooking.

'You look distracted. Why don't you try gardening?' says one prim, straight-backed individual. *You look uptight. Why don't you try shagging?*

She kindly gives me eggs with gunk on their shells. 'Organic!' she says with a smile. *Gross!* I think. But I say 'thank you' like all fee-paying pupils do. *But next time bring me Wotsits, not unborn babies.*

I now know the names of different cows, ranks and what a Right Honourable is. But I still can't do the country. I grew up in a flat with no balcony. Cars, not trees on the street. I am urban, made of concrete, full of fumes, not pure fresh air. The city is in my blood. *I really need to get out of here!* I have tried to embrace it, really I have. Yes, I know I have no traffic but I also have no life, I have alienated all around me.

So I lure my London friends to visit. They arrive in their blacked-out Range Rovers late on Friday and party hard till Sunday. Hung-over, they roll back into their beasts with their sunglasses on and roar into the traffic home. I wouldn't have minded them wasting all my lovely Cowshed products in the shower singing 'Wonderwall' badly for one night, but not for two. It's such hard work.

They don't normally travel outside Westbourne Grove, let alone the M25, so I was honoured, but I doubt I'll be seeing them again. My fair-weather friends. Fuck 'em, I hate anyone for more than an evening anyway. The only person I'll have to stay now is my mother.

House of Schmod
February 2009

She's never introduced and is always five paces behind, for fear of a fellow parent meeting her. Should I apologise for her aloofness? Explain away her detachment? Her lack of etiquette is obvious; easier to keep her in the car.

I want to be so proud of my mother, treat her with some respect. I used to, but sometimes I wish she was dead. Five years on from her recovery she's declining. Her pain too great, my sorrow too much, she's shrivelling in front of my eyes.

Here she comes, little Mrs Care-in-the-Community, with her flimsy wheelie bought in Fulham Broadway. I must buy her a Longchamp handbag to complete her smart-lady-from-Chelsea look. I pick her up at the picture postcard station and drive fast through the fields to home.

Back in my not-so-country kitchen she paces up and down, she doesn't like it here either. No cafes to pop out to, no charity shops to explore, she's caged in by all this space. So I take her to collect the children from school, something to do. Her medication doesn't stop her beaming when she sees them. Unfortunately, my daughter is not so bothered when she sees her, she outgrew her when she was two. My mother doesn't notice, thank God. She duly gives her huggles and kisses on demand.

As the weekend passes, I notice there is not much interaction between them. My mother sits very still by the window staring at the herons down by the stream until I give her an order. 'Help your grandchild put away her Lego. Give her a little hug. Now please read to her.'

'Rapunzel, Rapunzel, let down your hair,' my mother narrates flatly.

'Grandma, can I let down your hair?' my daughter asks excitedly.

'What a good idea!' I encourage. My mother responds automatically like an android and sits sedately as her plait falls away. Any traces of irritability have been drugged out of her. She is but a shell.

'But a shell of a grandma is better than no grandma at all,' I can hear my uncle Danny saying. It's for the best; the alternative is too dangerous.

I watch continually for signs of her illness returning. Do I hear a play on words? That's the first clue that she has missed her medication. Schizophrenics love to find dark hidden meanings where none exist. From 'water' she'll get 'ter', and before you know it 'ter, ter, terrifying'. Once, buying mangetout for supper, she came up with 'man get out'. If it wasn't so insidious it would be inspired.

The next clue that she has missed her medication is paranoia. The last, violence. She can't see my children if she's not topped up to the hilt and tranquil. These are the rules and they can never be broken.

On Sunday morning I decide to take her to the high-end Catholic church around the corner. She'll like that, I think. Once a place of worship for an uber-grand family, their descendants now make up most of the paltry congregation.

My mum is textbook Catholic, with her crucifix outside her black polo-neck jumper. Now cashmere, as I've upgraded her musty-smelling clothes. She's so religious that if there was a picture of the Pope she'd be kissing it. She has her own precious dog-eared Bible and makes the sign of the cross at every church we pass. I make the sign of two fingers, even though me and God are trying to patch things up. I have a long history with God Schmod, with my Catholic primary school, Catholic girls' private school run by nuns, then my Catholic girls' grammar. I walked to church practically every Sunday since birth. I was christened, confirmed, even won tickets to see the Pope when he came over in the eighties, but gave them to an old lady who'd be dead next time he came. She needed him more than I did, I remember thinking.

I am intentionally late for the service. I don't want to do small talk outside the grand portico with what turns out to be half my neighbours. They have kept their religious leanings quiet, I thought the country was full of Proddies, silly me. Posh Catholics from ancestral English families, I didn't know there was such a thing. I thought Catholics were poor and thick with no direction. I was wrong, there are rich and thick ones too. Perhaps they'll warm to me now they know I'm one of them. I won't tell them I'm lapsed.

We creep in and the beauty of the place startles me. Then I hear the Virgin's prayer. 'Hail Mary, full of grace, The Lord is with thee' and memories of childhood come racing back.

'Again,' God's helper ordered, 'Again!'

There is always a child worse off than me.

I feel sick, I'm determined to hate this House of God, so I try and find things wrong with it. 'It's free-ee-zing!' I whisper to my mum, as we sit down on a hard wooden pew. Not wanting to disturb the service we sit right at the back and listen to the priest mumbling on in monotone. I think he thinks he's being very interesting. I look about me. Does he not notice most of his followers seem to have fallen asleep?

Me being quiet lasts all of a minute as my phone goes off with its rapper ringtone. I ignore it and look around disapprovingly pretending it's not mine. Mum blows my cover, telling me to 'Shhh!' as she bends in prayer. *She seems quite lucid today.*

I can't do this. I'm about to giggle at all these earnest, self-righteous faces. I bet at least one of these old men dipped into the sex of an underage girl last night. *Hypocrites!* Then they have the nerve to ask God to forgive their sins this morning, so they can abuse the poor girl for another week.

Yes, you just keep on coming to church, old codger. Go ahead and have the body of Christ on Sunday, so you can go ahead and have the body of a little girl on Monday. You make me retch!

I leave noisily, banging heavy wooden doors behind me.

One day I'm going to get you. Insert a sparkler in your dick, set it alight and watch you scream. Just like when your kind watched me scream. You fucking cunt!

This is tiring; I have to stop thinking that everyone is a paedophile. I am becoming like my mother, for she wears a cilice too. Pills may have softened her itch but they'll never replace it.

All cats are black in the dark
June 2010

I am starting to regret having my tits done a size bigger than the surgeon recommended. 'People may notice,' he said. He was right. These country folk are obsessed with them. At least it stops them looking at my very expensive nose. Price of a car that op, but well worth it. When my friends go on about the size of my tits a little too much,

I start accusing them of being bisexual. They don't like that, and soon shut up. But they do still stare.

I never let them get changed with me by a pool, because they will see my scars. But they can't see the scars inside, just a well-moneyed mummy in front of them. A big smile but a tad demure.

I put my hands over my ears and leave the kitchen table when one of them starts talking about the latest child abuse scandal for fear I will throw up, cry and never stop; collapse and never get up again; for fear I will be found out for my tit job, my nose job, my Botox, my fraud, my destitution, my prostitution. My lies, my deceit, my life.

I like flirting with the odd man. The older the better, especially the clever ones; the bigger their brains, the wetter I get. But there's no 'throwing your keys in the bowl' round here. I wouldn't do anything anyway. I take my marriage vows seriously, being a good Catholic girl. Besides, all cats are black in the dark. There's nothing wrong with a bit of mental adultery every now and then.

I'm supposed to be a shy, retiring, scared, greasy-haired mouse, wearing baggy clothes and making-myself-look-as-ugly-as-possible-so-no one-will-violate-me type of person. That's how I imagine a textbook victim of rape. But I am not textbook and I'll do anything for kicks.

I like trying to work out which man is a paedophile, there must be one in every village. When I think I've found him, the one who stares too long at little girls, I take his photo and find his address. I know I'm not supposed to. *He's* probably not a paedophile at all, just an oddball, poor fucker. *Get me out of here! This paranoia is consuming me!*

My heart is in West London, that's my home. I want to go back to where I am celebrated, not tolerated. To find there's no parking space and be squashed into a house with no garden. I want to be with old friends, a clash of cultures and religions. Blonde and blue-eyed, black and green-eyed, red and hazel-eyed. Bronzed, pale, buff, fit, tight, taut. Spray-tanned, pushed-up, pushed-back, tucked-in, lifted, frozen. Wearing Chloe or McQueen, mixed with market-stall finds and exclusive sample sales, with exquisite jewellery and expensive hair. The very scent of these girls makes men explode. They are magnetic, sophisticated, atheist and so not posh. Girls so successful they transcend their class. London, the energy, the madness of it all. *Let me go home!*

Maybe I should obliterate Matthew before he obliterates me, then I will be free to go home.

The Fenian
October 2010

My father has been much on my mind. I've known his rough whereabouts for ages, thanks to my moronic uncle Danny. He's forever calling me about it.

'Will ya ever be seeing him?' My dad has been wanting back in my life since I had my children. Apparently he's dying to meet them.

'What, meet that deserter?' I reply. *Who left me to be abused.*

'Well now,' Danny replies, 'a da that deserted you is better than no da at all.'

My dad does not deserve to see me or be in my life, but the power of a blood tie takes over and I invite him down.

I am angry at my weakness, but curious and excited too. I drive to the station and meet him off the train. He comes down the platform, looking just like his pikey brother. He has a stoop, a crooked smile and the same mannerisms. He still has a full head of hair and twinkly pale blue-grey eyes, obscured by wonky glasses on a string.

I want to punch him, hug him, tear his eyes out. *For the life I had because of you.*

He likes a drink, a song and a chat about the Troubles. *I want to tell you about the hunger, the homelessness and the horror, Dad.*

He tells me stories of his adventures when he was younger. How he lost his hearing from a bomb. *How about I tell you when I lost my dignity?*

'There was smoke rising from the rubbish bin. Then the flesh and the blood came sailing past me. I saw myself screaming, my ears could hear nothing, I was moving in slow motion. All I could feel was the pain,' he says in a whisper. 'And since I had the Irish accent on me, I was too afraid to go to hospital, they'd suspect me, so they would.'

Like I give a shit.

'They suspected anyone who was Irish in those days, you know,' he continues. 'We were mercilessly hounded, harassed, beaten up, terrorised by the Brits.' He moves closer. 'When a bomb went off in Oxford Street, I was in my shop right opposite.' He stands up. 'It went *boom* right in front of me.' He closes his eyes and spreads his arms wide, looking like Jesus on the cross. 'The poor fella who perished, makes you weep, so it does. We all need emancipating, so we do.'

'Don't be comparing yourself to a hero now.' *You loser.*

He stands still in that position and tells me of another explosion. 'I was in Covent Garden when it went off, bloody frightening you know, just as well I was round the corner and not opposite,' he says, opening one eye for a second to check I'm still there. 'Those terrorists, they were animals, nearly killing their own kind, fecking eejits!'

'Bloody hell, that's quite a lot you witnessed, Dad. A bit of a coincidence, wouldn't you say? Always around the corner?'

'For fuck's sake, what are you insinuating?' he roars. 'I'm a Londoner, of course I was around the corner, all Londoners were around the corner from one bomb or another during that time. And where were you? That's right, around the bloody corner!' His temper is new to me, must be what my mum had to live with. 'Christ, being Irish doesn't make you guilty. You know I was held by the British and accused of being one of those terrorists myself?'

I raise an eyebrow. 'Methinks you protest too much, Dad.'

'Holy Mary, will ya not taint me by association as well? Your attitude reminds me of theirs.' He flops on the sofa and sighs. 'Jaase, you're far too anglicised for my liking. I'm surprised you're not singing "God Save Your Gracious Queen". You'll be burning your Irish passport next!'

'Have you finished your rant?' I reply, stone-faced. I can't let him know I'm faintly amused. 'Because if you haven't I could always put you on the next train home. Then there'd be no cosy bed for you tonight in your shitty bed-bug-ridden shack.'

He pouts and says nothing.

After some thought I say, 'You've got a point I suppose. I have in the past experienced hatred for our heritage myself. By rights I should be less suspicious of you, but I can't help but think there's no smoke without fire. You do have the same surname as a few fierce radicals after all.'

'You leave me well alone.'

'There is something suspicious about you, all right.' I continue with my bullying banter, enjoying taking the mickey out of a man who has no right to answer back.

He tries his best to ignore my comments and proceeds to tell me all he has to say on his past, yet I tell him nothing. He's had a colourful and loaded life, so have I. If I told him everything, he'd probably put his hands over his ears, curl into a ball and scream. Or maybe he wouldn't.

My boy adores him, my daughter is aloof. Quite why my boy has taken to him is a mystery seeing as how my dad just peers over his Irish newspaper and occasionally pats him on the head. He's rubbish with kids, has no idea. But my young son can tell that this old man with bent glasses and a mobile phone hanging from a string around his neck is somehow important in our family.

As my uncle Danny would say, 'A granda who's rubbish, is better than no granda at all.'

Eventually I can take no more and shout to my dad. 'What's wrong with you! You're in England now. If you want to carry on reading that Paddy paper, bugger off back to Ireland.'

'But most of my friends are in it,' he meekly replies.

'Yeah, yeah.' *So full of shit.*

I snatch it from him, throw it on the fire and give him *The Times*.

'Now there's a proper paper,' I say.

His nose crinkles up and he sulkily takes it, places it under his arm and slopes out for a walk, ending up in the local pub for a pint. Goodness knows what they think of him in there.

'Bet they checked under your seat for bombs,' I say, when he shuffles back for supper. 'You could do with smartening yourself up a bit.'

He looks and smells like a homeless man with his frayed blazer that slopes on the shoulders, his stained chinos and the boat shoes that I can see his socks through.

'Ah, I don't care about stuff any more,' he replies, looking down, wiggling his toe. 'I had the suit, the car, the hottest girl. I was one of the first with a car phone as well. Things mean nothing to me now, but I had to have them in the first place to realise that. I see myself more as a Buddhist than a Catholic these days.'

Dad, a tramp, more like. Just because you've stopped caring, doesn't mean you have to stop washing.

He's famished now and tucks greedily into my 'Irish' portions. Bland food but plenty of it, always swimming in gravy. I sit next to him. I can't help but like him, but I don't let him know it.

My daughter skips past in a leotard. His eyes seem to swallow her. After a pause he says, 'Her body is developing early.'

An observation not a question. Telling, from a man who never lived with children. My hackles go up, how would he know what a young girl's body is like? I am not going to let him forget for a second that he's in my life only because I've allowed him. 'And I can take that away in an instant,' I remind him.

He is on edge now. He wants to be invited back. He's becoming very keen on my boy.

'Grandpa is coming for Christmas Day!' I excitedly tell the children.

I have prezzies for him wrapped up under my ridiculously tall tree. A bloody expensive wine-opener from Harrods, he could do with it, seeing as he drinks so much; a cashmere scarf and a pair of Church's shoes, so at least he looks like a gentleman.

I drive like a granny through black ice to Trumpton Station. The train arrives through the darkness. Presents stumble off with passengers. Loved ones are greeted one by one by family. I wait and I wait.

Where are you, Dad? Behind that pile of Selfridges' bags? That box of tinsel? I search the smallest station in the world, peer into the waiting room, the loos, the scrubland. *Dad, did you miss your stop?*

He's not on the train, but I know he has a ticket because I bought the bloody thing. I go home worried. I can't reach him on his phone. I wait one hour before calling Uncle Danny.

'Jaase, I've been wanking about you!'

'What?'

'Cunt on a stick, who the *fuck* is that?' He's drunk.

'Your niece, you bell end, your niece! Who did you think it was?'

'Christ, raise me to fucking heaven, I thought you were my girlfriend!' He's cringing and we're both laughing now.

Shitebrain hasn't seen him. I wait till midnight and report him missing to the police.

I put his presents in the cupboard. They keep staring at me, asking, 'Where is he?'

I don't bloody know!

I take his place setting away. M&S ready-prepared Christmas lunch, how could it go wrong?

My uncle phones. Dad has been arrested and refused bail.

'The eejit is in prison pending a court case,' he says. *It must be serious.*

'Drink driving? Hit and run?' I ask, with heart pounding.

'The bleeding tosspot is in solitary for his own protection.'

Terrorism. The word shoots into my head and I can't get it out. I want to hear it from the boys in blue myself but they won't tell me anything apart from, 'We can assure you he is safe and well.'

'I want to know what he's in for.'

'If your father wants you to know of his charge, I'm sure he'll contact you.'

He doesn't and Christmas Day cannot stop because of bad news.

I plough through the festivities on standby mode, smiling because I have to. I take out my foil dishes from the oven and spoon slops of carrot and swede mash, two slices of bird within a bird within a bird, four roast potatoes and 18 sprouts.

'Too many? So sorry!'

It's a nut roast for me. I pour veggie gravy until it's spilling from the sides as usual, thinking of my dad. He liked my gravy. *D'you get Christmas lunch in prison, Dad?*

I'm in a bad way. I must hide it from the children, so after lunch we all watch the *Top Of The Pops* Christmas special and nearly make ourselves sick by doing silly dancing. Through my laughter I feel bitterness. I feel so duped. Those lies, that rant he gave me, 'I am Irish, not guilty,' he said. And I believed him! Those explosions he witnessed, were they the results of his own fair hands? There are just too many coincidences for my liking. I am pissed off with myself for letting him charm his way back into my life. For allowing myself to like him.

'Where is Grandpa?' my son asks. He will stop soon, I hope.

I spend days trying to get through to my hopeless uncle to find out if my suspicions about my father are true.

'A terrorist? Good God, no!' Uncle Danny cackles down the phone. 'The very thought of it. Your da was thoroughly security checked and eventually given clearance from Special Branch. In fact he was so low risk they asked him to be an informer.'

We get cut off. *Bloody mobiles!*

My mind is racing. An informer? I'm so relieved. I thought he was maiming people, not helping them. But I'm also confused, guilty even, about how I heckled him. What *is* he in for? For the first time in my life I feel sorry for the man.

'I can't believe he was an informer!' I say to Spudhead, when he finally calls me back.

This notion is hysterical to him. 'No, the gobshite never became a bleeding informer. His balls were not big enough for that. Your da told the goons to feck off. I know so I do, I was there. It takes a brave man to say to the enemy, "I'll not shit on my own kind." Your da was very calm when interrogated, you know. I was raging.

Your da told me after, "I wasn't worried, because I knew I was innocent. Come now, they're only doing their job." I then told your da we should complain.'

My uncle was now officially off on one. 'Jaysus, being innocent didn't mean shit in those days. It didn't help the Guildford Four, did it? My fellow countrymen were wrongly imprisoned for over a decade, that could easily have been us. Special Branch didn't like your da saying "no" to helping them, so they screwed him for something else – tax evasion. They even accused him of being the Paymaster General of the IRA!'

'So he's in for tax dodging?' I say, puzzled.

'Christ no, that was more than 30 years ago.'

'What's he in for then?' I shout impatiently.

'How the fuck should I know?' my uncle giggles. He thinks the whole thing is hilarious, hasn't had so much attention from anyone since he was a baba.

'You halfwit,' I snap. How can I take seriously a man who spends most of his nights in a shitty white van?

Shooting the messenger
January 2011

After an endless week of waiting, I finally found out what my dad was arrested for. I picked up my uncle from Notting Hill Gate Tube and parked round the corner in a residents' bay. Looking around my gas guzzler, my uncle's eyes landed on the TV screen in the dashboard, which showed the car behind.

'Would ya believe it. There's a camera in the arsehole of the vehicle.'

'Just get on with it,' I replied, opening my window, needing some air.

'Don't open the windows! No one must hear us or we'll be shot. Are ya hearin' me? Shot!' Uncle Danny shouted dramatically.

God give me patience with this ninny of an uncle. He does not give the Irish a good name.

'No phones, I said no phones,' he went on. 'They can hear you even when the phones are turned off.'

'Who is "they"?'

Ignoramus ignored me.

'Take out the battery in the back of your phone,' he said, 'that's the only way to beat them. I won't talk till it's done.'

Who the hell is 'them'? I am weary, give me rest.

'I am telling you, your father says it goes all the way up to the House of Lords.'

'What are you on about?' I said, puzzled.

'They'll kill him and then they'll make it look like suicide!'

It's time for him to go to the same hospital as my mother.

'What – are – you – on – about,' I repeated.

'He's a what d'you call it, a… paedophile.'

'What?'

'A PAE-DO-PHILE.'

'I don't believe it,' I said, shaking.

''Fraid so, the fecking cunt. Your da is saying he's innocent, of course. Weeping like a baby so he is, telling me he's a scapegoat for something much, much bigger. "I'm frightened," your da says. "They're powerful people in a ring protecting each other. And if I be spilling the beans, I'll be sure to disappear".'

'I can't bear it,' I said, still in disbelief. I preferred it when I thought he was a terrorist.

'He's a messer, so he is. Looking back, I always knew he was.'

'You *knew* he was? Why didn't you tell me? You let him come near me,' I cried. 'And my children!'

'Jaysus, Mary and Joseph, you can't go around accusing people of things like *that*!' Uncle Danny said, wounded. 'It's a very awkward subject.'

A coward. What do I expect from a man I caught jipping, who then gave me a tenner to keep me quiet. It's embarrassment that keeps paedophilia rife.

'Get out, go on, get out!' I shouted, pushing him into the rain.

'Heavens above, don't be shooting the messenger, will ya?'

Waves of terror. How could this be? Is this why my dad was so keen to come back into my life? Because of my kids? Or should I cling on to the hope that he is a pawn in a sinister game?

Dad,

I'm in disbelief. I just thought you were some harmless old man. That come six pm, you had a drink and didn't stop with your wine and cheese till midnight.

I am wired, I cannot sleep. Another wave.

I thought I was safe in my own home, the doors were locked, but you were right here!

Nameless children

The police now want to show me over 100,000 children's faces from indecent images they say they found on my dad's computers. 'To make sure they are not your children,' the officer said.

'*What*? He didn't go near my children!'

'It's okay, the bodies in the photos will be blurred.'

This is heavy shit. Who are they? Nameless children with blonde hair and rosy cheeks, red hair and freckles, brown eyes with curls looking straight at the camera. Bruised and abused, adults of the future. The suffering of little children. I want to fucking scream!

There are so many questions from the authorities about my father.

'Were you at any time sexually abused by him?'

'No.'

'Are you sure your father was never alone with your son or daughter?'

'Never.'

'Mm. We may want to talk to your little boy and girl.'

'No way.'

'You won't have a choice. Earlier you said your dad stayed one night when you were out. Now, I'm aware that you had a babysitter, but how do you know he did not go into your children's room?'

'Because he was intoxicated by alcohol and had gone to bed, that's why I had a babysitter.'

'He might have been pretending.'

'The guest room where he stayed is in a different part of the house. He would have had to walk past the babysitter watching telly to get to them.'

'We would like to talk to the babysitter and see the house.'

'No way.'

'Again, you don't have a choice. Did your father ever go near your children's school?'

'Yes. He went with me once in the car.'

'We'll need to talk to the school, inform the headmaster.'

I do it first, damage limitation. Oh, the humiliation! Then I call a lawyer.

I have a drink, *I can't handle this*, then I swallow Valium. *Why has this policeman's intrusive enquiries tipped me over the edge?* I do not understand. My mind is racing. Did my father touch his own grandchildren? No, no. I need not worry; they were never alone. I'm not rewriting history to cover up a terrible truth, I find comfort in that. This makes me feel guilty, so guilty. *Dear Nameless Children, whoever you are, whatever he did, no one is as sorry as me.*

Dad, guilty or innocent, which one is it to be? If you really are a paedophile, Dad, selfishly I should say thank you. Thank you for leaving before I was born, not being in my life, not abusing me, somebody else did that. But I think you are into boys anyway. You no longer have a granddaughter or a grandson. I am going to tell them that you are dead. DEAD!

'Dead? How can ya tell your wee girl and boy your own da is dead? That would be very bold!' cried Uncle Danny. 'You haven't yet given him a chance to explain himself, put things right. You never know, there maybe something in his protestations.'

'My dad had nearly 40 fucking years of chance! The day he left me was the day I severed all loyalty to my father. Come to think of it, the day my family left me to cope with my mad mother by myself was the day I severed all ties with you too. Never mind the children's home. I have no loyalty towards any of you at all. He is not my problem; you are not my problem. I owe him nothing, I owe you squilch.'

'But he's blood!' my uncle shouted, very distressed. 'That's thicker than water.'

'Blood may be thicker than water but not when it's poisoned,' I replied, bitterly.

Now desperate, Danny drivelled, 'Isn't blood that's poisoned better than no blood at all??'

God, give me strength.

'Children, I am so sorry, never again will you see your grandpa. Never again will you see your likeness, your crooked smile in a man who is your blood relative. Your grandpa has gone to a land far far away in the candyfloss clouds. Look up! You may see him, creating shapes with clouds to make a sign, make you laugh, make you remember.'

Dad, aargh, I can't do it! But what else can I say to them? The truth? 'Children, your grandpa is a suspected paedophile.' It wouldn't be fair to tell them that. They are words they wouldn't understand, words they don't need to know, words that would frighten them, the worst they could ever imagine.

Routine, routine, gotta have routine. But all I can think of is my dad's sentencing. When I talk to the mothers in the school car park I feel removed. I'm a mess and they don't know why. Never mind I'm an Irish Catholic, rumour has it I'm an alcoholic; there'd be less shame in that. The words are there but I cannot get them out. I've been here before. I find it hard to tell.

I sit in my 4x4 reading *Grazia* till the clock hits bang on 3.30. I only get out before time if I see an open minded mother, stay well hidden if I don't.

I need my dad's case to close to get on with my life. Crossing the playground I have an uncontrollable urge to shout, 'My dad is a suspected paedophile!' instead of 'See you at match tea!' The weight of this secret is making it difficult to have polite conversation. I feel as if I'm lying. But I'm not lying, I'm just not telling, there is a difference.

Teachers, when I pick up my youngest from class, please don't corner me in the classroom. I'll make sure my son has an immaculate uniform and a blindingly white PE kit. His hair will be tidy and his nails kept short. No food will be left at the corner of his mouth, no sleep in his eyes or dinosaur breath, but please don't ask me for more.

Please no, 'Bake us a cake, to help with the fete.' I am floundering.

Please no, 'Reading after school.' I am slipping.

Please no, 'Parents' meeting.' I can't make it. Sorry, I can't take it. I'm fucked in the head right now.

A bird in a cage
July 2011

Returning from a trip to Ibiza there's a message from my uncle Danny. 'Gobshite's court date is in October.' He hasn't remembered it's my birthday. Nor has my dad. Not a huge surprise.

Dad,

You could have at least sent me a birthday card from prison, or a letter, that would have been nice. What am I supposed to think when you say nothing?

21 September 2011

'I am telling you my fecking brother is guilty.'

'I can't keep up! You were on his side before.'

'Your da made money from dealing photos.'

'Where on earth did you pick that up from? Uncle Danny, you sound like you are talking out of your arse again.'

I feel the butterflies in my stomach, and not from a foetus, from fear. What if he really is guilty of the most unspeakable crime? My own father, those children. *Don't let it be true.*

'It's a big case, it'll be plastered on the front page of the tabloids,' my uncle warns me gleefully.

Mums, please don't taint me by association. But it will be too late. Clucking hens at the school gate will know and my cover of a normal middle-class mum will be broken. All I'll have left is stares, stilted smiles, whispers and zero dinner invitations. Strange, if I were still in London I'd be inundated. 'Obviously terrible darling, but simply thrilling, do tell us more over pudding.'

24 September 2011

I see a lollipop lady before I turn into school, I want to cry. Strange, I'm feeling so fragile, I'm crying at anything, listening to The Script doesn't help.

'Hello, hello, hello, hello,' to those same hundred faces. *Don't watch the news on 3 October, will you? My dad will be on it. Yes, you saw him once, remember? He smiled at you from my car.*

Palpitations. I don't want to think about it. I couldn't sleep again. I want this to be over.

27 September 2011

My father has lost his home and all his belongings. 'All taken!' Uncle Danny screeches.

I know what that feels like, but I can't feel sorry for a supposed dealer in kiddy porn. Uncle Danny witters on: 'But his type are given everything. Your da will get a flat in no time, you'll see. The council look after those sickos better than the teenage mammies.'

3 October 2011

Listening to Radio 4. Will the case be on? What will my dad get? On the news I hear a paedophile has been murdered in prison. My hearts stops, only to start again with disappointment: the name read out was not my father's.

Uncle Danny calls. Case delayed till 6 October. The frustration!

6 October 2011
Noon

Glued to the news, panic has set in. I am ready to run.

3.14 p.m.
Court 5, case started

I take Valium, just one. I need to calm my nerves. I have to pick my children up at four.
   Can I drive on Valium?

3.30 p.m.

The faces, broad smiles, big waves. Ten-second conversations with teachers, mindless banter with the mums. Paranoia has set in. *Why is everyone staring at me?*
   'Your dad is a paedophile! Your daddy is a paedophile! Your kids' granddaddy is a paedophile!'
   No! No! No! It's okay, they're staring at my leather skinnies and my gold boots.
   'Please can we go to the toy shop, Mummy?'
   'Of course we can.'
   'Mummy will give you five pounds,' I tell them both when we get there, 'to buy a few little toys as a special treat. One, two, three, four, five.'

My boy struggles with a huge Lego box. 'Mummy, is this five pounds?' he says with a sideways smile. Such a gentle personality he has, like my own once was; how hard I have become.

My phone rings. 'Guilty, 28 months,' Uncle Danny tells me.

Is that all? Why not 15 years? An injustice. If he comes out alive, he'll have nothing but freedom. Albeit it with no friends, no family, no money, no life. 'Hope that hunchback Irish cunt is killed in there,' I whisper. 'Otherwise I'll be killing him myself.'

'If he is, I'll be doing the River Dance on his grave,' Danny replies.

'And Uncle Danny, I'll be singing, "God Save My Gracious Queen".'

'You know, we are not being fair. Surely a da who is a paedophile is better than no da at all?'

'Oh, eff off with your cod aphorisms!' I scream down the phone.

I feel a tug on my coat. 'Is this five pounds?' my daughter asks, holding a bumper pack of pens, pencils and paintbrushes. 'Yes, darling,' I murmur in a blur.

Relief. It may be over, but I'm none the wiser. *Guilty, guilty of what*?

I could ask my dad, if I could bring myself to see him. But would he tell me? 'The computers they seized were *not* mine,' he protested to my uncle. 'I am innocent. Please believe me!'

'*Do we not know* what is he guilty of?' I ask Uncle Danny.

'His man in the suit said, "That's confidential, your father has a right to privacy".'

A right to privacy, I've heard that before.

Christ, maybe it wasn't my father's computer and he's a scapegoat after all. Perhaps his eyes following my daughter everywhere were because he adored her? Narrowing like that because he was squinting? Who am I kidding?

My children excitedly place lots of toys on the shop counter. Distracted, I pay a fortune and leave without my wallet.

I couldn't face going to the trial of my father. It took ten months to come to court and he never contacted me, which made me believe he was guilty of something. I know he wouldn't have wanted me to be there. I don't know why but I felt I should respect his wishes, I wouldn't have liked what I'd heard in court anyway. Too much information. Him sitting helpless in the dock, praying he would not recognise a relative in the public seating area. A bird in a cage with no control over who came or who listened or of the outcome. I guess that's what he deserved.

People are convicted of sex offences relating to children every single day. My father's crime was far too common to be in the newspaper. Unless a paedophile ring has been smashed, or the paedophile is high profile, there's not enough interest. And now my father is a convicted sex offender.

Obligations of a sex offender 2011:

- Register your name, address and vehicle registration with the police annually.
- Inform the police if you leave the country for more than three days.
- If you go on holiday in the UK for more than seven days, you must tell the police the destination and full address of where you are staying.
- Failure to comply is subject to imprisonment.

Dad,

Ask yourself, what is the point of living? If you haven't yet been killed by others, kill yourself. I remember you told me you'd once had a nightmare that you attended your own funeral. You said you stood right by your coffin but were unable to talk to anyone around you. 'I couldn't reach out, I was invisible,' you said. Nor were you allowed to touch. 'It was terrible. Just terrible.' A premonition?

It's very hard to mourn someone who isn't really dead. I have no closure. It's like you're lost at sea or something. I was thinking of having a kind of wake for you, then I could say goodbye. But Dad, I don't want to say goodbye. You are my father, but you are also a paedophile. Therefore I'm not allowed to feel anything for you but hate. So why does it hurt when I think of you? Nine months in and the anger I felt has turned to sorrow.

I'm ashamed because I want to be with you one last time. Shout at you for slouching on my white sofa with your stupid Paddy paper. Scream at you when you pat your grandson on the head like a dog. Curse at you when you drink the Châteauneuf-du-Pape while I put him to bed.

Later that evening, when I sat next to you, I showed you how to get your mobile with the cracked screen back on to its English-speaking format. You'd set it to German while drunk from the wine. That bottle was meant to be a present for me, you said. You don't have a clue about me. I can't stand wine, of any kind.

Let me smell your cheap soap on your newly shaven, scraggy face once more. There were fresh spots of blood on your frayed collar if I recall. You felt you had to make an effort for me, because the last time you were here, I told you the neighbours thought you were a wino.

Let me wipe off the yucky dandruff on your bobbled polyester knit embroidered with the words 'I love London'. It should have said 'I love children'.

Are you gay? Is that why never saw me as a child? Because I was not a boy? If I had been, were you going to groom me? Did you want to groom my son? You once asked, 'Do I embarrass you?' You do now. I heard that when you were a young man, you gently washed the arthritic feet of an old neighbour you hardly knew, then went home to beat your wife. My mother.

We had bad times because of you. But there is forgiveness and I have plenty of it. So much love, can't you feel it? Time, we do not have much time. But I can't see you, because of my darling son and daughter. I have to protect them, I have to protect myself. Dad, I know you have to go, but before you leave my life, let me see your pale eyes twinkling once more. See you giggling from my cruel ribbing. You don't mind laughing at yourself, do you? Funny how a person can have so many facets to their personality. The whole of you isn't a paedophile, just a bit. Why couldn't you have contained that bit, the bad bit, and we could have all been a family? Why couldn't you have got rid of those abnormal thoughts? Then we wouldn't have to say goodbye. Dare I say I love you? You don't deserve it, but I do. I deserve love, I've got lots and I'm giving it to you. There's a turkey dinner in my freezer with your name on it. It will sit by my daughter's placenta till I have the strength to chuck it out, the very last tangible reminder I have of you.

'Mummy, you know that grandpa, the one with the phone around his neck, can he come and see me?'

'I'm sorry, my boy, he's off flying in the candyfloss clouds now, on an adventure. Up, up in the sky. You can wave to him if you like.'

'Hello, hello,' my son says. Looking up, he waves. 'Tell him to come here, Mummy. Come here Grandpa,' he shouts.

'He can't, my gorgeous boy.'

'Why not? I want him to come here,' he says, crossly, searching the clouds.

'There he is! Do you see him?' I say, crouching down and pointing at a plane.

'Hello, Grandpa,' he says, following the plane with his eyes.

Holding him I say, 'You must wave goodbye now, not hello.'

His lip trembles, he starts to cry. So do I.

'Bye bye.'

I am haunted by the memory of little children howling in a home. The sound of my boy crying is like fingernails scraping on a blackboard. Alarm bells sound in my head and my brain screams, 'Abuse!' I am in my dark hole of depression longer than he is crying. It takes me time to climb out and forget. I put my hands over my ears and start singing. 'La la la la LA LA LA LAAA LAAA!'

Am I turning into my mother?

A danger to herself
December 2011

'I am you today!' my mother announces. She's delusional again, her hair flailing in the biting wind as she picks up poo in the lane.

Before she came to stay with us, she had gone to visit her ailing mother. She slept in that little box bedroom with the painting of the young girl with tears in the corner of her big blue eyes. Is that why she got ill again? Being back there in that room? Or is it because some unthinking eejit in my family told her that her ex-husband, the father of her child, is a paedophile?

'A man is in me!' My mother stares at her reflection in my hallway mirror. She turns. Her eyes are not hers, she looks as if she wants to kill me. I am afraid. I've not seen that look on her face for at least ten years. Pure evil.

'Are you my grandmother in my daughter's body?' she cries. 'Is that you?' These words she spews are not good. I don't want her around the children when she's like this. She's going to have to go home in the morning.

I lock her out of the main house and leave her alone in the annexe. I'll not be able to sleep otherwise. When I let her out the next morning, she manically does the washing up. Her loose hair falls in the sink as she scrubs each knife frantically. Holding one to the light she spits on it.

'I have ten different childhoods I don't want!' she shouts, as she holds her fanny as if to protect it. Her face full of hate, she bounds towards me, her eyes wild. 'So sticky, icky, *icky*!' she screeches, punching her stomach hard.

In desperation I ring my uncle. 'My mum isn't well, please call in on her when she gets back home.'

'You fuss too much, she seemed all right to me when I saw her a while a go. She's just eccentric.'

Uncle Danny is still in denial, like all of them. It makes

me so angry. 'If that's the case,' I point out, 'Why does her psychiatric nurse confirm my findings?'

I ring the crisis team in London. 'I don't feel safe with her near my children,' I tell them. 'She scares me. I fear for her safety.'

Following their instructions, I put my mum on the train home, hoping she doesn't kill any 'Fat ugly men!' on the journey. It's not easy monitoring her from 100 miles away. I need to go home.

On arrival in Chelsea she rings. 'There's a child who is me, growing up in the house opposite. I have to make her look *ugly* to save her!'

But Mum, the problem is, paedophiles don't just do it to pretty girls, they do it to all sorts. Paedophiles don't focus on the face, they focus on the accessible.

My life has been dedicated to my mother having at least half a life. I can do no more. She needs specialist attention. I call to let the crisis team know that she is back at her flat. My mother is now under their care, not mine.

Dear Grandma,

Do you know what happened to me in your house? D'you know what I think happened to your daughter too? I have no proof, of course, but the words she vomits suggest abuse. I blame you. The fallout has ripped into the next generation and now you are suffering. God is punishing you every single day by keeping you alive so you have to live with the regret of not protecting my mother while sitting in your tatty brown chair surrounded by haunting photographs of the rest of your children. Stilted smiles for the camera. Look, look, look at those pictures, Grandma!

In your back garden, always the same rose bush but not the same child. Growing up in front of the camera, dressed in their Sunday best. In the annual birthday photograph, your rose bush is thriving, stronger, wilder. But my mother looks like she's shrinking, she's smaller, weaker. Her heart-shaped face looking straight into the camera at you, brow furrowed. Troubled at sixteen. But here she is, aged thirteen, beaming. Was that before the messing began?

Here she is again, in white, she seems far too wise for her teenage years. Pale and sullen compared to the boys with their Cheshire Cat grins in their crisp confirmation suits, their chests all puffed out, they look so proud, with their slicked-back hair, shiny borrowed shoes, buttonholes and pressed hankies placed just so.

Who is the mystery baby placed by that very same rose bush? Lost in her pram, you can hardly see her. A granddaughter, given away. What luck! I now see her smiling on Facebook, with a real smile, because she was spared the darkness in this family.

Don't kill yourself, Grandma. Stay alive a little bit longer, so you can see me follow in the footsteps of my mother because of you. I hope you're having fun. Praying desperately to yourself that you'll die tonight, then finding yourself waking up and living another endless torturous day.

The clock ticks, waiting for 8 a.m., 9 a.m., 10 a.m., 11 a.m., 12 p.m., 1 p.m., 2 p.m., 3 p.m., 4 p.m., 5 p.m., 6 p.m., 7 p.m., 8 p.m., 9 p.m., so you can at last go to bed and die.

When you die, my mum wants your chair. What's so good about your tatty armchair? It looks shit, so what if it's an heirloom? I'm going to burn it.

And what of the successes in her family? My uncles are all of sound mind, until some of them drink. The darkness has not escaped them either, are some of them guilty of hearing my mother's cries when they were children? Closet alcoholics and depressives in denial, spilling snippets of telling data, while drowning in pints of misery? *Are they* tears of regret for not coming to her rescue? Embarrassment they got off lightly, freed from abuse because they were boys?

Law of Talion
January 2012

I can't bear the paraphernalia of life. A button, a safety pin, a dry-cleaning ticket, coppers collecting in the corner, calling out, 'Look at me, I'm a mess!' My mind is not settled till the offending items have been put in their proper places. A clean surface. Order. Control. I need control. I then tidy till I drop.

I'm only just holding it together. A woman in the country with a house, a family and that longed-for middle-class life, but for how long? The fucked-up me is bubbling under the surface. Cocaine has to remain a word from my past. I am afraid of what I might do if I lose myself to a line. I am scared because I am so agitated. I don't quite trust myself not to go absolutely mental. If I do I'll shag my friend's father that's for sure.

Sauntering through a dull drinks party, I am making polite conversation with not my usual crowd.

'Does your husband hunt? Shoot? Fish?' says a man who's wearing frilly knee-high socks. His wife's perhaps?

I so want to blurt out my mum's old turn of phrase, 'You look like a cunt!' But think it rather unfair, seeing as he's the host in traditional shooting garb.

'No, my husband does not hunt, shoot or fish.'

So fuck off!

I'd prefer to speak to the gundog snoozing by the fire than this offensive bore. I yearn to break out and go back to the life I came from. I roar off to KFC up the M3 for a steamy corn on the cob. With hot butter dripping, I lick, suck and dream of being with crude people I don't have to put on a stupid voice for, wear my hair in a certain way for, have to hold back on the swearing for, and only have the one fucking drink. For fear of what I might do or say if I have more. I yearn to be back with the coarse and pleasured by the wicked, who'll not judge me for my insults, my drugs, my whoring, my loathing. But I'll lose my family, so I won't. The one thing that's holding me together, stopping me from sinking, is my home-grown family.

Back at home, my children smile at me and remind me that there must be some kind of God. My children are my teacher. They save me from myself.

My gorgeous boy, you with your cheesy grin, your toy planes, obsessed by Playmobil. I love that silly walk you do, always the joker. My darling girl, that big smile, obsessed by any book. That hug you give, so full of meaning, always the carer.

I must not fly, drive fast, go skiing, do anything reckless or go off the rails and die. I'm going to wrap myself in cotton wool and play it safe till you've both fled the nest. So you too will be safe. All this madness cannot happen to you.

How to prevent my children from becoming mad:
No paedophiles.
No stress.
No serious bumps to the head.
No street drugs.
Which means no going out of my sight, no challenges, no parties and definitely no adventures. My poor kids have a boring life ahead of them then.

But this madness has overtaken me.
My daughter is not allowed sleepovers. *Who's with her?*
'Everyone else is allowed, it's not fair!' she cries.
Or play dates. *Who's there? Who's there? Who's there?*
Or days out. *Where is she? Where is she? Where is she?*
I have to let go; she needs a life of her own. *But what if, what if, what if?*

The fear has consumed me. 'No-o! Don't go in the garden.'

Who's out there? Who's out there?

Who's OUT THERE!

'That kind of thing happens elsewhere,' the other mothers say. They think paedophiles don't exist in our well-groomed county. I'm seething. They're so narrow in their outlook, so inexperienced in life. *Excuse me, it can happen anywhere.*

These mums have this ignorant idea that paedophiles wear raincoats, white string vests, have bottle glasses and pot bellies. Why are they not more aware? Do they put their heads in the sand because they can't cope with the reality that a paedophile might be on their own doorstep?

Mothers can't tell I'm a victim of abuse. Survivors do not have uniforms, we look like everyone else; we are invisible. I look at the people around me. I cannot tell if one of them is a paedophile because paedophiles do not have a uniform either: they look like everyone else, they too are invisible. But they are everywhere.

Mothers,

I am angered by your ignorance, your refusal to understand the truth.

Teachers and staff need CRB checks, what about fellow parents? What's a CRB check anyway? Someone could be a paedophile who hasn't yet been caught, their record clean. The parents are having a dinner party. Who's there? Your child is running round unsupervised because the parents are drunk. They don't notice who's put her to bed.

'Be still, there's a good girl, be still…'

I can recognise the signs, can you? Sexual molestation may only take a few minutes but it can change a child's life forever.

When you take your child swimming, a familiar face throws her up and down in the air. Her legs are round his waist, her feet are locked around his back. He is swishing her through the pool. Where is his left hand? Tightly holding her. But now it moves down into her creases. His thumb flicks her costume to the side and disappears into her, further and further. Withdrawing and pushing into her, again and again. All the while playing, laughing, swooshing her around and around. So much water, bubbles and movement, you can't see her discomfort from the side of the pool. You can't hear her whimpering. He continues, in and out, harder now, frustrated, wanting more. Later, he thinks, later. It's hot, so you let your girl take her clothes off. She runs to him and wraps herself lovingly around him, jumping up and down. Where are his hands?

He cannot resist her exposed genitals inviting him in. 'It's not my fault she's put it on a plate,' he says to himself. 'Parading in front of me like that. There's no real harm in it. I'm a man after all, and men have their needs. Little girls don't know what's happening to them anyway. They're only young. I make it a game, they like to be tickled, they think it's fun. I also make them feel nice. I clean them up and they soon forget. Then I move on to the next one.'

Don't let him supervise bath time, he will lather her with soap, paying special attention, right there. Prolonging the strokes, creating lots and lots of foam, then slowly shower her off. He takes out his pocket-size camera and asks her to play statues. 'Copy my pose!' he says, making her giggle. One leg up on the side of the bath, bending over, on all fours, on her back with her legs spread in the air. 'This won't take long!' he says, but he will have those photographs for life. Showing them to his friends, fantasising fucking her, building up his pornographic collection the more he supervises her. Maybe one day actually entering her and not just with his fingers, thrusting into her, enjoying her, ruining her. All the while you are singing away to yourself cooking his dinner. It took you 20 minutes, it took him only ten.

Potential paedophiles are everywhere. They don't all have yellow teeth and breakfast on their scraggly beards. He could be sitting next to you on the bus, making silly faces at your child, playing peek-a-boo on the train. He could be in the park, salivating as you have your picnic or playing with them on the swings. His mouth drying, his breath shortening, his dick hardening, as he watches your child's skirt rise as she climbs higher and higher into a tree. He lusts for a cunt with no hair, at last he has found one.

He strolls over, stares at her for a long time, then you. He takes her hand, scoops her up and helps her out of the tree when she tumbles. He returns her to you smiling, hoping you are single so he can enter your life and your daughter's.

He walks you and your little girl home. He's very nice, playing, 'One, two, three, jump!' with her. He lets you talk about yourself, he flatters you, flirts with you, finds out where you live and sees you again. You let him in, you feed him, you kiss him. He is in your kitchen, your living room, your bed. He is opening your legs, waiting for your child's, pumping your pinkness, waiting for your child's, coming in you, then, when you are distracted, he moves on to your child. 'Don't be scared now, sometimes it spits!'

Without him, you are lonely; with him, you're happy. Your child is broken, you ignore it.

Or do they have a stepdad? Have you chosen well? Are you sure? Is he really reading her a bedtime story? What can you hear? Laughter or crying? They sound very similar. Why don't you check? Don't you want to know? Are you afraid of what you will find out?

It will ruin my world, I'll lose everything, you think. *I won't rock the boat, I'm sure he isn't*. Years later your daughter is anorexic, depressed, some say suicidal. I wonder why.

Aargh! How sad that I think like this. Fathers, grand-fathers, uncles, friends, guilty because they are men. It's not their fault my brain is twisted, I can't tell good from evil. They are just men. I can't go on like this. I just want to be like every other mother, ordinary.

I may look normal, but I'm not normal, not inside. I have nasty filth in my head. I don't want it in my head. I want to smash my head into a nice marble fireplace, smash it to pieces. I want to butt my head hard through a window, so shards of glass will stab me. I want this filth in my head to go away.

GO AWAY!

And when this filth has gone, will I be you? Will I be well? Will I be normal? That's how you become normal isn't it? Wash away your sins of the past?

> *'But as for the cowardly, the faithless, the detestable, as for murderers, the sexually immoral, sorcerers, idolaters, and all liars, their portion will be in the lake that burns with fire and sulphur, which is the second death.'*
> *REVELATION 21:8*

This is me, don't let this be me!

If I had a sign on my forehead saying 'I was groomed as a child', might I be forgiven for being paranoid? Matthew made me like this. I used to be so soft, warm, open, loving, concerned and sensitive to humans and animals around me. He took all my kindness away. My confidence, my ability to empathise, my patience. The remains of my childhood.

I was never nasty before. But then after he abused me I pulled the legs off house spiders, one by one, till their bodies fell on the floor and I crushed them, ground them into the soles of my shoes. Nor was I violent. But then I wanted to hit my mum, again and again and again. Punch, kick, bite, scratch her until she was a ball on the floor. I wanted to stamp on her. I didn't know why.

I am angry, so angry. The idea of eating meat reminds me of Matthew. Forced to swallow his come. He laughed, as ten million sperm swam down my throat. He poisoned me.

I became so cruel.

Matthew, you made me like this. As I taunted these little creatures, I thought of them as you. 'Do unto others as you would have them do unto you.' You broke the Golden Rule.

'An eye for an eye, a tooth for a tooth.' I will follow the Law of Talion, I will not turn the other cheek, nor forgive you of your sins. Because I despise you. I will torture you. Keep you alive a long time. Suffering from the injury I have inflicted upon you. I will cut your dick off with a razor blade, to emulate the snuff movies you forced me to watch while fucking me.

There is blood pumping from the wounded man's vein, spouting from his groin all over the walls of the grubby bathroom. The man desperately tries to get out of the room and be saved. He becomes paler and paler. He grabs the cameraman and pleads with him to, 'Help me make it stop!' I hear the cameraman laughing and the dying man screaming, before he finally passes out from the pain. He slumps head first into the bath full of water. I watch him drown.

Matthew,

I wouldn't let you pass out from the pain, or fall into a bath so you can have the pleasure of drowning, being free. I would keep you awake by kicking you, keep you alive longer by cutting your dick just enough, to slowly drain it. And I will be the cameraman.

When you are weak and grabbing me, pleading 'Make it stop!', I will be laughing, just as you were laughing when I pleaded for you to stop. I'll let your pain carry on, like you let mine carry on and on and on.

I will enjoy your tears, like you enjoyed mine. And when you finally cannot move, I will turn your pathetic body over and start fucking you. Fucking you with a razor blade up your arse, tearing into you like you tore into me.

But I haven't found you yet. I guess I'll just have to wait to kill you, but there are others who will do it for me. There are plenty of haters. Mobs waiting, till they can catch one of your kind. Then they'll rip you to pieces like a fox caught by the hunt.

Got to be careful who I tell about you, some are less forgiving than others. A friend said he'd do the job for me. Kill you for me. His name was Micky.

We were in the same circle, that's how I met him;
Irish Catholics always find each other. He was slight
with a full head of grey hair, from drifting from
place to place no doubt. Sleeping on friends' sofas,
nervous, never settling, another 'hidden homeless',
I guess. Micky had a past, he kept it well hidden.
He was up for the craic, always messing. Skipping
and joking, how he roared. He didn't look like a
murderer to me. He didn't tell me till I told him
about you, then he dropped the bomb. With his big
blue eyes opened wide he whispered, 'I will gladly kill
him, I have killed before.'

Matthew, how I wish for a quiet mind. For your shadow
to disperse, my cilice to break. You are a Catholic and I
am trying hard to forgive you.

I am trying to forgive God, my dad, my rellies, the
council for letting me down. I don't want to be like this
any more, I want to be at peace, I want to be forgiven.
I want to say sorry to the baby I aborted. Sorry to the
innocent men I hurt. Sorry for being a bitch, a tease. I
want to be free.

I want to let all this grief go, float away like a Chinese
paper lantern. One for my loneliness as a child, it made
me so needy. One for my mother, the sorrow that mental
illness brings. One for the horror of rape and how it
destroyed me. One for each of my unborn children.

Up, up in those not-so-candyfloss clouds the lanterns
go. Five ethereal lights climbing higher and higher.

I feel myself lifting too. The weight from my body, disappearing. Forty years of sadness leaving me. I am lighter.

The elephant
April 2012

'My mummy sleeps a lot,' my boy said to his teacher.

Beautiful Boy, Mummy is going away for a while. I'm not feeling quite myself. I have a sore head, just like that time when you had a sore head, remember? You sniffed, you sneezed, you coughed and hid under a blanky with a fluffy hot water bottle and your favourite teddy. You then drank lots of yummy pink medicine, watched cartoons and ate cookies till you were better.

So Mummy is off to the finest hospital in the land. I'll hide under my blanky too until I get better. Because I have a big naughty elephant stuck inside my head. You can't see him, he's invisible. You can't feel him, but he's always there. He's making my head quite heavy, that's why you see Mummy not getting out of bed for days and days and days.

He's very clever, that nice doctor at the hospital. He's going to pop the naughty elephant out. He will give Mummy some yummy medicine, just like yours, and it will make that naughty elephant come out. The elephant will pack his trunk, my mouth will open wide, and 'pop!' he'll be out! He'll then tramp down the road and be gone forever. No more elephant inside Mummy's head any more and Mummy will be better again.

'The sooner I go to hospital, the sooner I'll be home. Don't worry my boy, when have I ever not come home?'

My daughter was having so much fun at school, she shrugged her shoulders when I told her I was going away for a bit. I just had to store her teddy up with a few of my hugs first. 'So I can have a cuddle from you whenever I want one,' she said. Good idea.

I'm scared, I don't want to go. Do I really have to go? NO.

Day after day, I lay in bed listening to the laughter of little ones below and the happiness of my own children made me better. I came down in my dressing gown and the cry of 'There's Mummy!' made me weep at what I'd been missing. Week after week their smiles made me melt, their cuddles made me stronger. And the weeks turned into months as I said by rote, *life is good, life is good, life is good!*

String of pearls
October 2012

I'm well now. I can hear for one, I had a test. There is nothing wrong with my hearing, it was all in my head. The stuff that was happening to me, I just didn't want to hear. I was nasty before, now I'm serene. But I'll always have a little sting. I'll never be perfect.

People can't tell from the outside that I'm at peace. Perhaps I seem slightly softer, calmer even.

I let my daughter do sleepovers now. It would be selfish of me to stop her because of my irrational paranoia. It still feels as if I've left the iron on, though, when she's not here. I'm constantly waking, panicking, praying she's safe. The fear of rape stays with me.

Dear Blue Peter,

Am I allowed a badge now? I am not expecting a gold one or anything like that, I'm aware they're very hard to get.

'Only awarded for really outstanding achievements like showing amazing bravery or courage.' Not bravery or courage but I have balls, will that do? I forgot, I haven't shown it, my achievements are invisible, I don't need a gold badge to know what I have overcome.

I found out from a drunken uncle why my mother was such a snob. She had been born into wealth and privilege. Her early childhood was made up of maids, money and material things. She lived in a fine house lost by her gambling father, whose family had in turn lost their childhood home to the Black and Tans. A very Irish story. One that explained her nose in the air and refusing council flats not in Georgian houses.

With the money gone, my granda left my grandma and his brood homeless. My grandma moved across the water into a house she previously wouldn't have looked twice at.

My mother grew up and married beneath her, or that's what I imagined. But it turns out that my father is an Irish gentleman. Not that you'd know to look at him, dishevelled as he is. He went to the Irish equivalent of Eton. So did Uncle Danny. Christ, they're hardly great adverts for such a fine establishment. I mean, respected Irishmen of note were educated there. No wonder my father knew everyone in the Irish papers. I'm surprised he kept that quiet. He usually liked to brag.

My dad's father put all of his children through boarding school in the fifties – quite a feat. He shouldn't have bothered, mind. When my educated dad and his brothers were trying to find work in London in the sixties, the English were so anti-Irish, the only job they'd give them was digging the Victoria Line.

There were more relatives, some more affluent than others. There was no need for me ever to be in that home.

'Jaase, if I'd have known, I'd have taken you in!' said Uncle full-of-shit.

But you did know; you chose not to. 'Uncle Danny, go fuck yourself.'

I feel sick, my life is a joke. I could have been not poor from birth, like Little Miss Alice Band. She might have played with me then.

For years I thought there was no point telling my rellies what had happened to me. The weight of them knowing would be too much. I purposefully distanced myself so the subject would not arise. Now I don't care whether they know or not. I feel that they are the evil that fed me to the beast.

My Irish roots I abandon, my relatives I divorce. Uncle Danny, Brendan, Fergal, Hugh, Dylan and my dad, Johnny. Auntie Nora and Una. I am wiping the slate clean. I will take myself out of the past and look to the future, that feels good to me. I now have the courage to tell my husband all, to face up to his judgement. I will risk our marriage because nothing is real without the truth.

When I tell him everything Josh looks at me for a long time. Then he says: 'I used to jokingly say, "You can't choose your family, you can't choose your wife either." But you swept me up and made life happen. And here we are with two gorgeous kids ten years later, so you can't be that bad. Marni, I knew all along that your flat was council, your accent fake, your clothes mostly cheap, your tits made of silicone. But I didn't care because I loved you, more than your long toe, I just didn't let on. If you choose to tell me more, I will still love you. Because I may not have known about your past but when I met you I could feel your strength. I knew it would carry me through life. "For better, for worse, for richer, for poorer, in sickness and in health, until death do us part." That's why I married you.'

And with that he handed me a string of real pearls.

As for my friends, I'll tell them every detail and finish by saying, 'Remember, I am still the same person you knew an hour ago.' And if they choose to continue to know me, I'll feel happy and say, 'You are my true friends.' But if anyone turns me away, I can only say: 'I am sorry if I've offended you, but I can't feel any more shame. I punished myself for so long I'm tired, I don't want to hide any more. This is who I am.'

> *Dear Children in Need,*
>
> *I'm so sorry. So sorry Wogan. I was angry, alone, confused; I needed to blame someone, so I blamed you. That was wrong. Children would be much worse off without you. What you do every year is amazing. I now have annual parties for Children In Need, with the programme proudly blaring in every room. Wogan wittering on in my dining room, joking in my kitchen, laughing with me loud in my living room. If you can hear me, Wogan, I'd like to say, 'My life is wonderful now, but I'd still like to see the show.'*

I found out my dad was around more than I knew when I was a toddler. Did he do things to me? I don't know, I don't remember, I don't *need* to know.

My mind violently intrudes placid thoughts, projecting sickening scenarios in 3D, throwing me back into the dark.

In you go, in you go now. See what has gone on before.

I cannot see my father, but Matthew is in Technicolor.

I haven't seen Matthew since that day in the Portobello road but I know he is still alive. I console myself with the thought that he's too old to work with children now. I've decided to embrace his existence and return to London. I'll not be afraid, I am an adult now, the law will protect me from him. I will not let his presence in this world hinder me, prevent me from living my life. If he wants to find me he can. And face me.

King's Cross Station
December 2012

Can you feel her happiness? The girl with blonde hair and blue eyes? She turned double figures last birthday. Dressed warmly in Uggs and a cashmere covering her healthy frame. Smiling while waiting for her mummy to return with chocolate croissants for the train. On holiday at Christmas, she skips off down the platform with her mother, father and little brother. A nice normal family.

The girl raises her hand to her chest. She is confident, she is strong. She is not ripe pickings, ready for an abuser to pounce. For this is not a child in need, this is my beloved daughter.

I look at her and mourn for my innocence lost. I have given her the life I would have loved. The fact that she knows nothing else is the achievement I'm most proud of. In her and my son's life there will be no more madness.

I now like Christmas, like this happiness I am feeling. I have a home, a family, cornflakes and freshly squeezed orange with the juicy bits, if I fancy it. I have the chaos before leaving for the school run in the morning. 'Where's your coat? Your toothbrush?' I holler at my kids, drowning out Radio 6. I don't need to go to sleep and wake up in January, because I've accepted who I've been and got used to who I am: a woman liberated, a skank no longer. I'm now a warrior.

After a life experience like mine, I can't just sit back and drink champagne, I have to do something. Speak out for others, because I don't want others to become like me, their bodies experienced before their minds are ready. Knowing their first time was their worst time. Bored by boys because they're used to men. I will talk about it and I won't stop talking about it until people start listening.

If you're in the room, made to look, forbidden to leave, you might understand, feel the horror, want to help, make it go away.

Good must come out of bad.

Author's note

If you are worried about a child, don't wait. You can anonymously contact NSPCC: nspcc.org.uk.

Stand tall. Show courage. Break the silence. Unite.

Acknowledgements

A very big thank you to the gorgeous Mark McCrum, who mentored me throughout this book. To my editor Charlotte Cole, who made me feel good about myself. My trusted agent Andrew Lownie. And my husband who never doubted me.

To my mother: I wish you could start your life again, for there can be joy in childhood; I see it through your grandchildren.